BORN OF
WATER,
BORN OF
SPIRIT

BORN OF
WATER,
BORN OF
SPIRIT

SUPPORTING THE MINISTRY OF THE
BAPTIZED IN SMALL CONGREGATIONS

Sheryl A. Kujawa-Holbrook

Fredrica Harris Thompsett

THE
ALBAN
INSTITUTE

Herndon, Virginia
www.alban.org

The Alban Institute
2121 Cooperative Way, Suite 100
Herndon, VA 20171

Scripture quotations, unless otherwise noted, are from the New Revised Standard Version of the Bible, copyright © 1989, Division of Christian Education of the National Council of Churches of Christ in the United States of America, and are used by permission.

Material developed by the Episcopal Diocese of Vermont on pages [Intro sidebars, ch 2 sidebars, figs. 2.2, 2.3, 2.4] is used by permission.

Material developed by the Episcopal Diocese of Northern Michigan on pages [ch 2 sidebar, fig. 2.1, 2.4] is used by permission.

Cover design by Spark Design.

Library of Congress Cataloging-in-Publication Data

Kujawa-Holbrook, Sheryl A.
  Born of water, born of Spirit : supporting the ministry of the baptized in small congregations / Sheryl A. Kujawa-Holbrook and Fredrica Harris Thompsett.
    p. cm.
  Includes bibliographical references (p.167).
  ISBN 978-1-56699-400-2
  1. Lay ministry–Episcopal Church. 2. Small churches. 3. Baptism–Episcopal Church. I. Thompsett, Fredrica Harris, 1942- II. Title.
  BX5968.K85 2010
  253–dc22
                                          2010002653

10   11   12   13   14   VP   1   2   3   4   5

To our teachers, mentors, and companions on the journey:

Lynne Wilson, 1944–2006
and
James Arthur Kelsey, 1952–2007

CONTENTS

FOREWORD

You have in your hands a remarkable book designed for congregational and diocesan (judicatory) study. Here is both a manual and personal account of how widely diverse and dispersed congregations and judicatories are reexamining Christian living through the lens of baptism, water, and the Spirit. I believe you will be fascinated by the who, what, where, how, and why of mutual baptismal ministry. Experiences and principles emerge from unbelievably diverse sources—both geographically and denominationally.

This rediscovery of baptismal living is bubbling up in all sorts of places differing by context, but common in their relationship to our roots in baptism. One of the signs that a movement is of the Spirit is how widely separated the promptings of the Spirit are and yet how common their basic features are. Therefore, we need not reinvent a movement, but instead apply these experiences to our context to strengthen our denominational and local practices.

There is a Sufi saying that one can only learn what one already knows. As you study and reflect on the experiences of this book, look for and anticipate occasions where you will spontaneously say, "Oh, I know what that is—what is being described." Where the information corroborates with your experience and your hopes, there pursue your common insight more deeply and intentionally.

My experience of mutual ministry in the Diocese of Northern Michigan has spanned some twenty-eight years as bishop, as a retired member of the diocese for eight years, and now three years as assisting bishop as we seek a successor to Jim Kelsey, our dear bishop and close friend who died suddenly and tragically as he was returning from a Sunday visitation.

In my experience, a key to pursuing baptismal living is to have a diocese that understands the relationship of the adult baptized to the ordained members of the diocese and congregation. Let me present a view of ordered ministry that I have learned firsthand and that is liberating to the ordained. Baptism undergirds every ordination, whether of a bishop, priest, or deacon. What's more, each of these orders points to, prods, and symbolizes responsibilities shared with, and enlivened by, the adult baptized.

A deacon is ordered to serve and raise servant ministry with the church gathered. Yet 90% of our life is lived at home, at work, and among neighbors. What the deacon can do on a Sunday pales when compared to calling the baptized to address servanthood at home, and in all times and places. So the profound responsibility of the deacon is not to do our servant ministry for us, but to identify and lift up the remarkable ministry of servanthood among the baptized.

A priest is ordered to symbolize the ministry of reconciliation, raising up the necessity of forgiving and being forgiven, and breaking down barriers that dehumanize relationships. A priest presides at God's table where our unity, our reconciled life in Christ, is known in breaking bread together. Yet we live within a ferment of conflict within our schools, homes, councils, and we find national and international conflicts on our news broadcasts. So the ministry of the priest is to lift up and publicly affirm the rich ministry of reconciliation unfolding among us, yet so often unrecognized and unappreciated—because it does not happen in Church.

For example, some years ago in Ironwood I was reflecting with members of the Church of the Transfiguration about what today I would call baptismal living. A woman saw a connection between her work and our conversation. She said she drove a school bus every day. Often there is conflict among students early in the morning. Recently she described retaining two kids as the bus emptied. She told them to resolve their conflict before they boarded the bus to go home and that, if they could not come to a resolution, she would help them. She then asked knowingly: "Was that a priestly ministry of reconciliation?" Beautiful and powerfully so, I concurred.

Bishops in my denominational family are ordered to symbolize the ministry of oversight, study, and witness. In leadership we weave congregations of the baptized into a geographical unity of life and vision. Similarly, bishops remind and encourage us to accept positions of oversight and leadership within our local and wider communities. The bishop's apostolic leadership confronts us with the needs and concerns of the world. As a bishop, I have experienced a rich ministry of oversight enlivened by the adult baptized in their homes, work, and communities.

Sharing the responsibilities of ordered ministry with the adult baptized is not based on delegation by a central figure. My successor, Jim Kelsey, referred to this as a "one man band" where in the name of mutual ministry the rector passes out the drums to this person, the piccolo to another, someone else received the trombone, and whatever else is distributed to the delight in the congregation. This is not mutual ministry or baptismal living. This only clericalizes the few, and never leavens the loaf.

Those of us excited about mutual ministry and baptismal living must be very careful. To think we finally have it right is seriously arrogant. There is a danger in any effort of renewal when we are very dissatisfied with where we are and think where we are going is God's true plan. Of all the various and sobering gifts Paul identifies in 1 Corinthians 12, he concludes by saying "strive for the greater gifts. And I will show you a still more excellent way." Then in chapter 13, he remarkably identifies the gifts of faith and hope and love. And we know which of these is greatest. So we realize that deeply, richly embedded in baptismal living are these three gifts—universally shared in some significant measure.

The three orders of ministry reflected and represented regularly in each congregation echo our Trinitarian roots, which are essential to our theological roots. No one person has it all and individuality is only completed in unity, in community, and in communion. Here collaboration is essential. Here God is revealed and baptismal living is undergirded. This is the mutual ministry identified and honored in this book with many expressions emerging in varying contexts. Thank you Sheryl and thank you Fredrica.

Thomas K. Ray
Retired Bishop of The Episcopal Diocese of Northern Michigan

ACKNOWLEDGMENTS

Friendships nurtured in community are at the heart of all ministries. This is particularly true of those engaged in the ministry of the baptized where relationships are trustworthy in large measure because power is shared. This project began among friends. Many people, congregations, and communities have graced our paths over the past years with hospitality, wisdom, and enthusiasm. The Episcopal dioceses of Maine, Vermont, and New Hampshire were our partners on our first grant to strengthen the ministry of the baptized. The circle later expanded to include the gifts of the dioceses of Northern Michigan and Wyoming, the Scottish Episcopal Church, and then wider still to other dioceses: Utah, Minnesota, West Virginia, and Olympia in Washington State to name a few. Members of the collective called the Living Stones Partnership from both Canada and the United States offered advice and support. Those who shaped educational materials from the online resources *LifeCycles* and LeaderResources as well as members of the Ministry Developers' Collaborative were unfailingly helpful. All of you have made an impact on our lives and on this book. You have been our teachers and mentors. We are indeed privileged to be learners in your midst, witnesses both to the struggles and the vibrancy of your mission. What we have been able to present in this book is intended as an introduction to your stories, stories that continue to grow and be conveyed to others interested in shared and baptismal ministry. Your passion for sustaining and extending Christian community is contagious. If, along the way and out of zeal, we have misconstrued your exact situation, the fault is ours.

We could not have accomplished this study without the support and encouragement of an institution that sets high standards for ministerial leadership. Colleagues associated with the Sustaining Pastoral Excellence Program of the Lilly Endowment, in particular John Wimmer, program director, have graced and informed our wisdom for close to a decade. You have guided us from the start and turned us again and again to wider visions of leadership. John, you have reminded us that one person can make a difference, especially when that person insists on working alongside and valuing others. We remain very grateful for a second grant to support and sustain this work for an additional three years through the Pastoral Excellence Program at the Episcopal Divinity School (EDS).

The Alban Institute supported this book from the beginning, and published earlier forms of this work as articles in *Congregations* magazine. Special thanks go to Richard Bass, director of publishing, and Marlis McCollum, former managing editor of *Congregations*, for their skill and patience.

The seminary community of EDS in Cambridge, Massachusetts, has supported and embraced our enthusiasm for baptismal ministry. Faculty colleagues and students have expressed in several ways a renewed appreciation for small, vital congregations. Chris Carr, Liz Magill, and Julie Lytle have labored with insight and expertise to extend our efforts. The Conant Fund administered by the Episcopal Church Center and the EDS Theological Writing Fund have provided valued financial support.

Among these and others overflowing with baptismal grace, the loving support of our families stands first and foremost.

BORN OF WATER,
BORN OF SPIRIT

The first place of Christian belonging for many is the baptismal font. Yet the words that are spoken and the symbolic actions that take place as we are born of water, born of spirit, are understood in a variety of ways. This book focuses on the variety of ways people in small congregations are living out their baptism, and the impact of baptismal living on congregations, judicatories, and the wider communities they serve.

What does the church look like if it takes the ministry of the baptized, the priesthood of all believers, seriously? How are congregations transformed when the church supports and affirms the ministry of all the baptized? What difference does it make in the way we understand all ministry? The ways we prepare people for ministry? What is learned from models of baptismal ministry recovery and enrichment—a theme that deeply undergirds Reformation convictions about the priesthood of all believers? Can we use the challenge of taking the ministry of the baptized seriously as an opportunity to more fully and faithfully incorporate the gifts of all in the life and ministry of the church? How does the recovery of baptismal living and ministry revitalize small congregations, particularly those in insolated and often poor communities? What configuration of ecclesial structures and educational models need to emerge in the next decades to assure not only survival for these congregations, but also vitality?

The Faith Communities Today project of the Hartford Institute for Religion Research states that 53 percent of the mainline Protestant congregations in the United States have fewer than one hundred regularly participating adults and 75 percent are located in small town and rural settings. A full quarter of small congregations have fewer than fifty regularly participating adults, while only seven percent of mainline Protestant congregations have more than 351 members. The study also states that 21 percent of these congregations have no full-time staff at all, while another 53 percent employ one full-time person. Religious education is of the utmost importance in small congregations, with 90 percent reporting that it is "almost as foundational as worship."[1]

The focus of *Born of Water, Born of Spirit* is on small congregations, most of which have fewer than fifty regularly participating adults, many of which are in rural communities; some are in isolated and poor communities, and all are in the midst of deep change. Deep change is different from incremental change in that it is discontinuous with the past; it involves new ways of being, thinking, and action, as well as taking risks. It requires us to walk outside the comfort of traditionally prescribed roles and "to walk naked into the land of uncertainty."[2] The small congregations and judicatories whose stories are part of this book are in the midst of deep change. They have recovered their sense of purpose through reaffirming the ministry of the baptized, and through this process are redefining previously accepted norms about viability, leadership, and the role of the church in their communities. These small congregations provide vital ministries for their larger communities and, in so doing, have made the boundaries between church and society more porous and more flexible. Members of these small congregations have learned to redefine ministry to include ministries exercised in daily life, rather than restricted to those conducted under the auspices of the church or directly related to church maintenance. Local leaders are raised up for ministry in these congregations, some for ordination, others for ministries as educators or as pastoral caregivers, or in community service. Although some of the congregations studied in this book turned to supporting the ministry of the baptized out of financial necessity, they have since come to appreciate that the enrichment goes far beyond economic need and, in fact, revitalizes the whole congregation. Effective judicatory support to these communities is based in resource development and forms of governance that value the distinctiveness and leadership of a given congregation.

FOCUS ON BAPTISM

Baptism is deeply grounded in the generosity of God. Like all other biblical covenants, whether the Hebraic covenants of Noah, Abraham and Sarah, Moses, and Jeremiah or the new covenant proclaimed by Paul and others, baptism is a response to God's initiating love. The influential reformer Martin Luther wrote that baptism is "so great, gracious, and full of comfort, we should diligently see to it that we ceaselessly, joyfully, and from the heart thank, praise, and honor God for it."[3] Another influential reformer, John Calvin, asserted that "baptism is the initiatory sign by which we are admitted to the fellowship of the Church, that being ingrafted into Christ we may be accounted children of God."[4] Today we who are born of water, born of spirit, are called forth like our biblical ancestors, summoned to lifelong relationship with God. A. Theodore Eastman, the retired bishop of the Episcopal Diocese of Maryland, in his hymn on baptism, "Holy and Creative Spirit," recalls the Holy Spirit as the one who redeems, anoints, renews, and embraces all out of the waters of baptism (see page 4).[5]

The theological foundation for baptismal living is grounded in the expectant hope God holds out for us. Resting on this solid base, baptismal living is pursued in humanity's hope-filled response of seeking God's reign and expressed in the persistent hopefulness of daily living. As the traditional hymn text asserts, "All our hope on God is founded." The sacraments of baptism and Eucharist are filled with hope because they strengthen and encourage us to look toward the future rather than feel resigned to the past. The liturgy, wherever it takes its substance from the gospel, "is the festival of life which foretells the fulfillment and maturity of all life for all of time in this time," writes William Stringfellow. "All baptized people, whatever their work or rank, location or function, charismatic gifts or personal talents, share in the one ministry of the body of Christ for the world *in* the world."[6] Christians are now paying renewed critical attention to baptism and to the formative, hope-filled theological foundations of this sacrament.

Two contemporary shifts account for the renewed interest in baptism throughout the Christian church, one liturgical and the other societal. One major perspective for change is evident in the positive ecumenical and denominational achievements of the modern liturgical renewal

HOLY AND CREATIVE SPIRIT

Holy and creative Spirit,
    source of all primal birth:
Out of uncorrupted waters
    you brought forth earth;
As crown of your creation,
    you breathed all flesh to life.
Stir up our will to keep your world
    from wanton waste and strife.

Holy and redemptive Spirit,
    liberating power:
When your children were in bondage
    in their darkest hour,
You guided and released them
    beyond the parted sea.
Break the chains that fetter us;
    see every people set free.

Holy and anointing Spirit,
    calling some apart:
After Jesus rose from Jordan,
    you enflamed his heart;
You sent him forth with Good News
    for those with many needs.
Raise up today a servant church
    to follow where he leads.

Holy and renewing Spirit,
    working in us still:
Through Baptism's cleansing water
    you forgave self-will;
You raise us to a new life
    with the eternal Son.
Help us to affirm the victory
    which Jesus Christ has won.

Holy and embracing Spirit,
    reaching out for all:
In your ceaseless, surging rhythms
    we have heard your call;
You fill us with your music
    and send us forth to sing
To humankind throughout the earth;
    Let peace and justice ring.

—A. Theodore Eastman, 1975;
new text by Eastman, 2009. Used with permission.

movement of the 1960s, which has restored baptism to liturgical prominence and made it a focus of religious identity. Liturgical renewal during the second half of the twentieth century offered contemporary Christians the opportunity to renew their theological understanding of baptism. The Christian understanding of baptism has moved from a private, domestic celebration of a moment in an infant's life to promises that are publicly made, shared, held, and affirmed in gathered community amid individual lifetimes of godly living. We are moving away from patterns that obscure the fact of God's goodness in creation. In the ecumenical arena, as affirmed in the World Council of Church's 1982 text *Baptism, Eucharist and Ministry*, baptismal theology has shifted from an emphasis upon the stain of original sin to the promise of new life in Christ. We no longer ask, as we did in the past, "What happens if the infant dies?" Today we might rephrase the question to ask, "What happens if the infant lives?"[7] Whether the candidate for baptism in a parish today is an infant, a youth, or an adult convert, contemporary preparation for baptism holds meaning for life. For all participants—candidates, godparents, sponsors, and the community gathered to witness and support baptismal promises—the gift of baptism extends life-changing implications. Ecumenical theology suggests that the fundamental authority for ministry occurs through baptism as full initiation by water and the Holy Spirit into Christ's body, the church. As Orthodox Metropolitan John Zizioulas writes, "all are ordained in baptism."[8]

Today, violent religious divisions and genocide in many parts of the world have brought a second shift that impels us to reexamine religious formation in baptism. The Holocaust changed the shape of theology, underscoring the problem for Christians and Jews alike in speaking of God "after Auschwitz."[9] That forty-five million Christians were also martyred during the twentieth century—from the Armenians executed for their faith early in the century up through the eight hundred thousand Tutsis massacred in Rwanda toward the century's end—is a startling fact.[10] In these and other massive outbreaks of genocide, religious identity and religious rhetoric have been used to polarize and divide. With such compelling claims upon our attention in communities of faith and within the wider global community, we dare not fantasize or become nostalgic about religious rites of initiation. Nor is it biblically honest to hold privatized religious commitments that are blind to the suffering of others or that are otherworldly. Nor, in this increasingly multifaith world, can people of any faith hoard God's generosity in one religious tradition. In such hard times, attempts to speak honestly about formative religious identity today carry a critical urgency that encompasses multifaith visions of reconciliation.

For Christians, baptism provides an optimistic and hopeful orientation that paradoxically situates us amid human suffering in the world for which Christ died. Anglican liturgical scholar Louis Weil strongly advocates the renewal of baptismal theology as a foundation that will allow us to "coexist with other world religions" and with those who are indifferent to religion as well.[11] Weil, among others, calls for the renewal of a baptismal ecclesiology that is effective liturgically, socially, and globally. *Born of Water, Born of Spirit* speaks of theology from the standpoint of hope as it is embedded in baptismal living, liturgically represented in covenental promises, expressed in ministry, directly attentive to evil and suffering, and open to dialogue with people of other faith communities.

BAPTISMAL MINISTRY AND PASTORAL EXCELLENCE

In 2002 EDS received a five-year grant from the Lilly Endowment to develop resources under the auspices of the Sustaining Pastoral Excellence Program for underserved congregations in northern New England. This book is the result of we authors' learning for this five-year period and beyond. The Lilly Foundation graciously extended the original five-year grant for an additional three years. The focus of the Sustaining Pastoral Excellence Program at EDS is the recovery and enrichment of the ministry of the baptized in small congregations in underserved regions as a means of revitalizing the church in these communities. Throughout rural New England and other regions of the United States, Canada, Europe, Australia, Southern Africa, and the world, there are small congregations uniquely qualified to serve their communities but traditionally underserved by denominational programs. Many of these communities are remote and poor and find it difficult to attract and retain seminary-trained clergy. In the same communities the possibilities for substantial numerical growth are slight.

For instance, many small communities along the North Atlantic coast of the United States and Canada have been negatively affected by the collapse of the fishing industry, leaving whole towns without jobs or prospects for economic recovery. Those who are able to move to other regions for work, including young people, are forced to do so, leaving behind the elders and family connections generations old. In such congregations, growth is not as effectively measured in numbers as it is in the depth of commitment to pastoral care or in the growth in members' prayer lives or in the degree of giving to the wider community. Although not considered viable congregations according to criteria focused on ability to sustain seminary-trained clergy, such congregations respond to the ministry of the baptized deeply and effectively in their contexts through the ministries of local leaders.

Further, the Sustaining Pastoral Excellence Program at EDS looks for ways denominations and seminaries can more effectively support these small and vital congregations. In the belief that no community should be without pastoral care or the sacraments because of an inability to pay professional salaries, this book looks at the importance of supporting the whole people of God not only for ministry through the church but also throughout their daily lives. The Sustaining Pastoral Excellence Program at EDS first developed partnerships within our own region of New England and the Episcopal dioceses comprising the states of Maine, Vermont, and New Hampshire. Beyond this regional focus, the project has partnerships with the dioceses of Northern Michigan, Wyoming, and Western Newfoundland. We have also worked with church leaders in Alaska, California, Connecticut, Maryland, Massachusetts, Nebraska, Nevada, Tennessee, Virginia, and Washington State; in Quebec; and in Scotland in the United Kingdom. In addition, organizational partners for this work have included the Living Stones Partnership and LeaderResources, both organizations that work throughout North America to provide resources and support for ministry development in traditionally underserved communities. Although our original partnerships were contracted through the Episcopal Church, the project has worked ecumenically, particularly with the United Church of Christ, Disciples of Christ, and the United Church of Canada. While our initial focus was on rural and often isolated contexts, the project has also invited participation from small urban and suburban congregations interested in enriching the ministry of the baptized in more traditional church structures. Given the realities of small congregations "on the ground," our project by definition has had to work ecumenically, and our learning has ecumenical implications. Certainly, the authority of baptism should not be limited by church politics, although one negative result of denominationalism has been to limit the ministry of the priesthood of all believers. Yet small communities are fertile ground for ecumenical perspectives on ministry because these congregations more naturally work together out of shared need and culture. These smaller congregations often have more in common with each other across denominational boundaries than they do with corporate congregations of their own denominations. Thus, *Born of Water, Born of Spirit* is a book geared to a reality where ecumenical participation is a value as well as a necessity.

Some Definitions

Just as baptismal ministry is responsive to local contexts, so the two of us have discovered during the course of the Sustaining Pastoral Excellence project at the EDS that the definitions related to this work vary across local congregations, judicatories, and denominations. For instance, terms such as *total ministry, mutual ministry,* and *local collaborative ministry* share the theological assumptions of *baptismal ministry* and in some cases are used synonymously. To provide readers with some clarity, the two of us offer the following definitions, hoping that others will intentionally amend this list as needed:[12]

Baptismal Living

The term *baptismal living* refers to baptized individuals living intentionally as the reconciling presence of the body of Christ in the world. The concept of baptismal living asserts that baptism is a gift, a reminder, and an invitation that changes who we are as well as how we live in the world. It is about living consciously and sacramentally as a member of Christ's crucified and risen body. Throughout this book, the term is most frequently used in the Episcopal Diocese of Vermont, where *baptismal living* is defined as the "committed response to live out our baptismal promises within God's Creation so all may be aware that we are in communion with a Living and Sustaining God." In this context, baptismal living is the fullest expression of a person's commitment to the baptismal promises, including ministries in daily life.[13]

BAPTISMAL MINISTRY

Baptismal ministry is discipleship where all baptized share in Christ's identity and mission as the priesthood of all believers. Through baptism each person receives gifts for ministry through the Holy Spirit—gifts to be embraced and lived out in the church and in the world. Baptismal ministry maintains that the calling of each person is of equal worth and essential for the fullness of mission—that is, to restore all people to unity with God. Baptismal ministry maintains that the local community is the primary context for formation, ministry, and mission. Beyond the congregation, baptismal ministry encompasses the whole work of the whole people of God in all times and all places. Verna Dozier, a biblical teacher and advocate for the ministry of the baptized, writes that we are "the church gathered and the church scattered."[14] Although at times unrecognized, the baptized are always the church in mission.

COVENANT GROUPS

Covenant groups engage in a period of prayer, discernment, and study on the way to becoming a ministry support team (defined below). During this period, the group explores the concept of baptismal ministry and invites members of the entire congregation to identify gifts for ministry, many of which are already at work within the community. Within the covenant group, members discern a call to ministry and then enter into a covenantal relationship with other group members that focuses on the norms of group life during their initial formation phase.

LAITY OR LAY

The *laity*, or *lay*, is from the Greek "laos," meaning "the people." The terms refer to "the whole people of God," or "the baptized." For those congregations and judicatories actively involved in baptismal ministry, the trend is away from using the terms *laity* or *lay* in a way that infers a negative or second-class status. In some contexts the term *nonordained* is preferred on those rare occasions that a distinction needs to be made. Rather, the baptized are all called to ministry as ambassadors of Christ in the world; each calling is of equal worth and essential for the fullness of God's mission.

LEADERRESOURCES

LeaderResources is a publishing and consulting ministry that began in the Episcopal Church but now serves many denominations. The resources are developed by congregations or dioceses, and then shared. The materials are practical and user friendly and have been tested by people in real congregations and judicatories. The materials are "evolutionary" in that they are constantly being added to and improved by all the people who use them. Many of the resources are downloadable. The resource *LifeCycles* is distributed through LeaderResources. Congregations and judicatories may sign up for memberships and receive discounted materials. *LifeCycles* is an integral approach to ministry development for adults, empowering all members to realize their gifts and to transform congregations into vital ministering communities. The process is built around four areas, including personal transformation, skills development, congregational or community formation, and systems change.

LIVING STONES PARTNERSHIP

Living Stones Partnership is a cooperative of more than twenty North American Anglican and Episcopal dioceses and faith communities engaged in developing baptismal ministry. The partnership gathers annually to share learning, joy, challenges, and resources. The partnership supports the Ministry Developers Collaborative, a group that provides training, education, and consultation for individuals and groups engaged in developing baptismal ministry.

LOCAL COLLABORATIVE MINISTRY

Often used synonymously with the term *baptismal ministry*, *local collaborative ministry* refers to the development of self-sustaining congregational life built on the ministry of all the baptized. In this book it is the term most frequently used by the Scottish Episcopal Church. Local collaborative ministry encourages church members to claim their discipleship, participate fully in the life of their faith community, and embrace ministry in their daily lives.

LOCAL ORDINATION

Local ordination refers to the process whereby a local congregation discerns an individual's gifts for ministry and call to ordained ministry. In many cases these people are also trained and mentored for a congregational role within their local context and their ministry is unpaid. Though denominational and judicatory policies vary within the Episcopal Church, local ordination is not commonly transferrable to other congregations.

MINISTRY DEVELOPER AND MINISTRY DEVELOPMENT

Ministry developers are people who support congregations in developing the ministry of the baptized and in the transition from dependence on professional ministry to a community where ministry is owned and shared by all the members. Some ministry developers work in clusters, some in mutual ministry or total ministry settings, some as judicatory resource staff, some as pastors of congregations. These people carry different titles in various settings: missioner, regional vicars, ministry enablers. Their role is to be a companion, teacher, and mentor rather than a pastor-in-charge. They are members of the baptized, including but not limited to the ordained, who focus on reshaping and building up ministering communities. Ministry developers draw upon a set of skills that stress consulting, networking, learning, and working with change, rather than directing, delegating, informing, and maintaining. *Ministry development* is, then, the answer to the following question: "How does the church in these contexts form our church members for effective Christian mission?"[15]

MINISTRY SUPPORT TEAM

The term *ministry support team* pertains to a group of people in a local congregation who have been formed and trained, then commissioned or ordained to support congregational members in discerning their own ministries, both inside the church and throughout daily life. Members of the team are identified by the local congregation and put forth as public ministers who provide the primary leadership for the congregation. Depending on location, this term is used synonymously with the terms *local ministry support team, shared ministry team, circle group,* and *ministry development support.*

Ministering Community

Rather than referring to communities gathered around a minister, *ministering communities* are congregations where the gifts of every baptized Christian are recognized and affirmed. At the heart of this vision is the belief that God has given sufficient gifts to each local congregation to enable the ministry and mission to which they are called. The term reminds us that the whole people of God are called as a community to continue the ministry of Jesus as his body, the church in the world.

Ministry Team

A *ministry team* is a group of people from a congregation or group of congregations, selected and called locally for specific ministries. Ministry teams typically include roles such as preacher(s), pastoral care minister, religious education minister, outreach and evangelism minister, stewardship minister, community life minister—all supported by a ministry developer or other mentor. The local congregation identifies the specific ministries the team is called to fulfill. Ministry teams may also include those individuals identified for local ordination by a congregation.

Missioner

Within baptismal ministry development, a *missioner* is an individual who provides resources, encouragement, and support in a region, for multiple congregations, or at the judicatory level. Typically, missioners have a formal role as judicatory staff. Some contexts have a bias toward ordained missioners, although whether all missioners need to be ordained is a matter of debate.

Mutual Ministry

Mutual ministry, often synonymous with *baptismal ministry* or *total ministry,* is a term used to encourage God's people as they share in the one ministry—that is, as they share in Christ's ministry. At its very core is the understanding that all Christians are ordained to ministry at our baptism and that ministry is a way of life. Thus, *mutual ministry* describes the shared ministry of all baptized people. It encourages us to move away from a primary focus on the ministry of ordained clergy and includes all the people of God in the mutual work of ministry. In this book the term is used most commonly in relation to the Episcopal Diocese of Northern Michigan.

REGIONAL MINISTRY

Regional ministry refers to a group or cluster of congregations yoked for ministry development, sometimes sharing paid missioners, clergy, or ministry developers.

SHARED MINISTRY

Shared ministry is a way of structuring ministry so that the local church is responsible for establishing priorities for mission and ministry. *Shared ministry* recognizes that every member is a minister and all the baptized have gifts. This is used synonymously with *baptismal ministry* and *mutual ministry*. In parts of New Zealand it is referred to as *shared local ministry*.

SPIRITUAL FORMATION

Spiritual formation is a lifelong process whereby individual believers grow spiritually, deepen their faith, and discern their vocation in the world. This process is aided through religious education, spiritual practices, and ministry development. Within the context of baptismal ministry, intentional spiritual formation for all is foundational.

THEOLOGICAL EDUCATION

Although the term *theological education* is traditionally used in reference to seminary education geared to the formation and education of clergy, within the context of baptismal ministry, the emphasis is on lifelong education for the entire faith community, rather than a privileged few. While traditional models of seminary education remain an important resource for all sorts of congregations, small congregations often feel neglected or misunderstood by theological educators and denominational bodies. Delivery systems that would make theological education more accessible to people on the local level need enhancement; congregations and judicatories involved in reviving the ministry of the baptized are also involved with designing alternative models of theological education for the whole people of God.

TOTAL MINISTRY

At the heart of the understanding of *total ministry* is the belief that through baptism all Christian people are gifted for mission and ministry. The "total ministry movement" refers to a paradigm shift to an understanding of the church as primarily a "ministering community" rather than "a community gathered around a minister." Total ministry as a concept began in remote Anglican contexts worldwide and has gained more exposure within other Christian and Unitarian faith communities. In some cases, the term is used synonymously with *baptismal ministry*. In others, such as the Episcopal Diocese of Northern California, the term more specifically refers to an action strategy, including the concept, processes, and curriculum used to revitalize congregations by developing baptismal ministry.

Throughout the book, we refer to various types of clergy roles common to Episcopal congregations: canon pastor, deacon, priest-in-charge, rector, and vicar. Although their definitions vary by diocese, the following general definitions may be helpful. *Canon pastor* is a title referring to a member of a bishop's or cathedral staff charged with pastoral care. In Episcopal usage, *deacon* refers to an ordained minister with a special ministry of servanthood directly under a bishop. Deacons assist bishops and priests in worship, the ministration of Word and Sacraments, and carry out other duties assigned by the bishop. A *rector* is a priest in charge of a local church or parish. *Priest-in-charge* refers to a clergyperson in charge of a congregation or cluster of congregations. *Vicar* is an English term referring to a clergyperson appointed in charge of a small congregation or mission.

BAPTISMAL MINISTRY
- Every Person
- Every Gift
- Every Ministry
- For Mission

From "Deepening Baptismal Ministry," The Episcopal Diocese of Vermont, 2007

THEOLOGICAL FOUNDATIONS FOR BAPTISMAL MINISTRY

As the research for this book indicates, the concept of baptismal ministry is defined in different ways in various contexts and is responsive to the needs of those communities. One helpful and concise definition for *baptismal ministry* is from the Episcopal Diocese of Northern California: "When we speak of baptismal ministry we refer to our lifelong engagement as the members of the Church of Jesus Christ, living a life of love of God and love of our neighbor for God's sake in Christ."[16] The diocese further offers the following principles as a basis for baptismal living:

- The Church, the body of Christ, exists to carry out God's mission
- Ministry happens in all of life's endeavors
- Learning in ministry begins with preparation for baptism and continues until death; it is experiential and lifelong
- The Gospel must be engaged afresh in every context, in every time and in every place
- Every person has a unique configuration of gifts; no one is omnicompetent
- No person is indispensible; every person is irreplaceable
- The Spirit equips every congregation with what it needs to do what God is calling it to do
- Congregations are not problems to be solved; like individuals, each has a unique pattern of gifts and opportunities which shape its ministry; ministries are not slots to be filled
- The local congregation or community of faith calls people to offices and specific ministries

The Episcopal Diocese of Vermont emphasizes the importance of "baptismal living," and how that calls the baptized into new ways of being and acting in the world "as the sacramental presence of Christ's body." Thomas Clark Ely, bishop of the Diocese of Vermont, envisions baptismal living as transformational. "We are eager to learn more. We are open to new experiences, and we have placed our trust and confidence in one another. We know we can learn from one another. We encourage one another, and we sometimes get nervous. We know that we need to sharpen our skills. We know that we need practice. We know that we need to go deeper into the water. And we are willing to do all those things because we love the water of baptismal living, and know that going deeper holds the promise of greater joy."[17] Ely writes of his own experience of baptismal living:

> For me, baptismal living is all about being and living in the world as the sacramental presence of Christ's Body. I have come to understand the water poured upon my head and the sign of the cross traced on my forehead in baptism as an incredible gift. Each morning when I look into the mirror I look for that cross as a reminder of who I am and whose I am. Buried with Christ in death, I live with Christ in resurrection. Not only does that change me, it changes how I live. That is baptismal living. . . . I recall someone once describing the baptismal font as the womb of God. What a wonderful image! It is the fluid of divine life that sustains me, helps to form me, gives birth to me and ultimately transforms me. Living as a member of Christ's crucified and risen body is the sacrament of baptismal life.[18]

The theological emphasis in baptism is based on God's action, expresses God's hopeful interest in humanity, and reveals God's generosity in creation. Baptism in the Christian Church (Disciples of Christ) tradition affirms a loving God "who created the world and who binds Christians in a covenant of love to God and to each other. Through baptism into Christ and Communion of the Holy Spirit, all are called together to discipleship, witness and service."[19] The neoorthodox theologian Karl Barth is said to have remarked, "God is omnipotent, God is omniscient, and now a few words about baptism." Theologically, it is important to recall that in baptism, as in creation, the baptized are bearing God's energy and Spirit. Baptism is not simply or only an individual decision; it is primarily

---

BAPTISMAL THEOLOGY

- Baptism gives us a part in the Church's life and *mission—restoring all people to unity with God and each other in Christ.*
- Baptism admits us to Christ's *priesthood.*
- Ministry, through baptism, is done *in community by all members.*

(From "Deepening Baptismal Ministry," the Episcopal Diocese of Vermont, 2007)

---

about God acting and the community of faith responding. God's doing calls forth our responsiveness. Baptism is an expression of God's hope for a people: created, chosen, and adopted anew as God's own. New Testament scholar L. William Countryman described baptism as interpreting "the gift bestowed in birth." The sacrament of baptism reaffirms and renews the holy character of creation. It expresses God's continuing engagement with, and hope for, humanity.

Appropriately, our response to God in baptism requires an affirmation of faith. The Apostles' Creed is a historic baptismal statement of the church that recalls Jesus's life, death, and resurrection and affirms God's triune nature. "By God's gift and call, all of us who have been baptized into Christ Jesus are daily put to death so we might be raised daily to newness of life," states the Evangelical Lutheran Church in America's (ELCA) view of baptism.[20] Then as now, each time a baptism takes place in a congregation, members are more than observers, witnesses, or even sponsors; all are able to renew their faith in a God who extends a new covenant of hope to humanity. "It makes no difference whether you were baptized as an adult or child; we all start on that journey of baptism," cites a United Methodist pastor's understanding of baptism. "If you experienced God's grace and were baptized as an adult or received baptism as a child and desire to reaffirm your baptismal vows, baptism still marks the beginning of a journey in the nurturing fellowship of the caring, learning, worshipping, serving congregation."[21]

In addition to affirmation of faith through the creeds, baptism calls us to reflect on the consequences of faith that we express and encounter in daily living.[22] What kind of responses will each of us make in our daily lives? There are many different and appropriate ways to explore the implication of baptismal commitment in daily life. Missiologist Ian Douglas, for example, points to baptism as a covenant for the baptized to engage in mission.[23] In her book *Living Water*, educator Klara Tammany provides multidimensional pathways for adult formation built around baptismal promises,[24] while Deborah Flemister Mullen, on faculty at McCormick Theological Seminary, describes baptism from an African American perspective as a "sacrament of struggle."[25] Throughout this book, baptism is framed as a covenant of hope, which accords biblically with God's overriding purpose in offering humanity a future and a promise. Even in times of serious displacement, as presented again and again by the prophets, God's hope is for the long haul, not for a quick fix or a fast "return to normalcy."[26] The first letter of Peter, sometimes described as a sermon on baptism, proclaims "new birth into a living hope" (1:3).[27] This is an ongoing process. Baptism does not rest alone on a past promise made by us or for us by others, nor is it a pledge to ensure our future security. Hope is the basis for our present and continuing response, our responsibility to God. As such it bears repeating. Sara Maitland, a Christian feminist theologian, underscores the nature of this responsibility: "Hope lies rather in accepting that God's engagement in the creation gives us not just the right, but the obligation to create and sustain the future. . . . Hope is the basis for taking responsibility: for claiming our capacity to create, to make a genuinely new thing. It is also the springboard for trying to act justly, and for accepting absolutely our incorporation into each other."[28]

Beyond participating in Sunday morning worship, baptism invites each one of us to be daily participants in living hope. Fortunately, we are reminded of this responsibility to take hope each time a baptism occurs. We are not left alone or without resources for this journey in hope. Accordingly and appropriately, baptismal living requires a commitment to lifelong religious formation through worship, prayer, Bible study, and life together in community. The nourishment that comes through observing the holy routine of the church year and participating in word and sacrament are primary ways that we continue to participate in the apostolic life. Yet just as worship is not the whole of the church's life, regular Sunday attendance is not the whole of religious formation. "Sunday school" is not, nor was it ever, only for children as it is in some congregations, or only held on Sunday. Educator Verna Dozier, one of the most provocative instigators of the ministry of the baptized asserts that, "religious authority comes with baptism."[29] If the baptized, including laity as well as clergy, are to claim their authority in church and in society, continuing study of Scripture and tradition, as well as attentive knowledge of contemporary life, is required. Baptism signals that God has important work to do. Through our baptism we commit ourselves to replenishing resources for this journey through worship, prayer, and study.

Further, participation in our baptism demands that we remain vigilant against sin and evil as individuals, in relationships, and throughout the world. "In baptism, God works in us the power of forgiveness, the renewal of the spirit, and the knowledge of the call to be God's people, always," states the United Church of Christ.[30] Baptismal living demands that we acknowledge directly the reality of systemic evil and individual sinfulness, repent, and return to God. We are called to resist external forces of evil as well as repent personal sins. The baptized, in the early church and in today's perilous times, live in a world marred by violence and suffering. Through our baptism, all Christians are called to actively address this condition with hopeful language of forgiveness and resistance. It recognizes starkly that no social transformation is possible without personal transformation. Repentance is multidimensional and ongoing. Active, not passive, response is called forth, as is perseverance over the long haul. This lesson applies to biblical times as well as to our own. Prophets and other theologians have long recognized the need for reshaping hope in new situations. This is clear in Jeremiah's response to the exiles: "I know the plans I have for you, says the LORD, plans for your welfare and not for harm, to give you a future with hope" (Jer. 29:11).[31] Augustine may have had resistance in mind when he noted that "hope has two lovely daughters—courage and anger."[32] In our own day, Martin Luther King Jr. often quoted words attributed to Edmund Burke, "The only thing necessary for the triumph of evil is for good men to do nothing."[33] Vincent Harding, an African American historian and activist who has told the story of the North American freedom movement, hails the "human potential for resistance and hope."[34] All of this and more is summed up by the baptismal injunction to persevere in resisting evil and in the call to repent and return to the Lord. The ELCA view of baptism stresses that through baptism "God delivers us from the forces of evil, puts our sinful self to death, gives us new birth, adopts us as children, and makes us members of the body of Christ."[35] This baptismal promise puts the decision to respond to evil and sin in our hands. This is strong religious medicine, just the sort of prescriptive affirmation needed to undergird hope among God's people in times of suffering, violence, and genocide.

Scripture tutors the baptized in exemplary living and a call to service. The baptized are sent into the world to serve in God's name. Again, this commitment to service is neither meant to be tamed nor is it meant to be confined to Sundays. The request here is not for volunteers. It is, as God's adopted own, to follow Jesus. Baptismal living does not simply mean "being good volunteers."[36] Verna Dozier bluntly asks, "Do you want to follow Jesus? Or are you content just to worship him?"[37] The call to discipleship, to service in the world, is neither a private call nor a call for the faint of heart. It is for the baptized, the collective, steadfast body of Christ sent forth in the power of the Spirit to perform the service set before them. Such service rests on the biblical, hope-filled promise of abundant gifts for ministry, like the many charisms named in the Pauline epistles.

The call of the baptized to committed service is demanding. Loving our neighbors may well prove costly. As Archbishop Desmond Tutu of South Africa repeatedly reminds audiences today, the people of God are meant to be Godlike, which we show in particular by loving our enemies. German theologian Dietrich Bonhoeffer summed up the role of the baptized in his book *The Cost of Discipleship* as a stance that embraces suffering as a universal part of the human condition in which God is also present. In Hitler's prisons, those who sought and received Bonhoeffer's spiritual guidance were not only fellow inmates but also prison guards. Hope comes with the recognition that suffering is part of the human condition and God embraces suffering fully. "Baptism calls us to hope in God for more," states an official document on baptism from the Presbyterian church. "We baptize in the strong name of the Trinity. God is not only our Creator. In Christ, God is also our Redeemer. As the Holy Spirit, God is also our Liberator and Transformer. As Christians we are not left to resign ourselves to the natural limitations and possibilities of our world, our culture or our individual tendencies."[38]

As in Scripture, baptismal hope emerges from the perspective of neighborly love amid the powerless and marginalized. One of the church's earliest baptismal formulas signified God's promise of freedom and unity in Christ. Paul envisioned baptism as overcoming all that separates human beings from one another and God: "There is no longer Jew or Greek, there is no longer slave or free, there is no longer male and female; for all of you are one in Christ Jesus" (Gal. 3:28). An implicit message is that cultural diversity discloses God's creativity. Paul's promise of baptismal unity in Galatians is expansive as well as inclusive. F. D. Maurice taught that God's redemptive love was intended for all, including those of other religions. The explicit intention of baptism is to call all Christians to respect the dignity of each person and culture, and baptism commits followers of Christ to justice and peace throughout the world. It is a boundless promise.

Today, as in biblical times, religious divisions ostensibly militate against peace and justice among people of different cultures and faiths. Dare we live with hope in today's world? How might a vow to seek justice and peace among all people become part of daily living? One story about seeking God's shalom comes via a colleague who participated in a church-sponsored peace mission among Palestinians. He reported stories of those who insisted that hope was a luxury they could no longer afford. A banner displayed at a massive demonstration for peace poignantly noted: "Due to present circumstances the light at the end of the tunnel has been put out." What happens if hope seems lost? What then is the responsibility of the baptized? Katharine Jefferts Schori, the presiding bishop of the Episcopal Church writes, "In baptism we discover that we are meant to be for others, in the same way that God is for us. This means that God's mission must be the primary focus, not anything that focuses on our own selves to the exclusion of the neighbor. For when we miss the neighbor, we miss God."[39] The baptized do not stand alone but are supported and upheld in the prayers of the whole community. "Let not . . . the hope of the poor be taken away" is a daily petition in Morning and Evening Prayer. The Psalter offers comfort, as in the opening verse of Psalm 46, "God is our hope and strength, a very present help in trouble."[40]

ASSUMPTIONS INFORMING
BORN OF WATER, BORN OF SPIRIT

Through over seven years of partnership with congregational and judicatory leaders who are trying to think outside the box, the Sustaining
Pastoral Excellence project at the EDS has had an opportunity to better understand the needs of small congregations, rethink ministry, assess
theological education for these contexts, and reflect on the role of the
church. That our theological thinking is not totally new is obvious, and
yet the project has given us an opportunity to engage in an intentional
way with local leaders on subjects integral to the future of the church.
Some of the theological assumptions that inform the Sustaining Pastoral
Excellence project at EDS, and thus informing *Born of Water, Born of
Spirit*, include:

- God is working within all people . . . infinitely more than we can
  ask or imagine
- God has already given us the gifts to lead the church into the
  future, if we are prepared to discern our ministries and have the
  courage to live them out
- Church means Christians, the people of God
- Baptism, not ordination, shapes the church's identity and mission
- Baptism is primarily about God acting and the community of
  faith responding; it shapes our primary identity as members of
  Christian churches
- The authority for ministry comes with baptism; though laity and
  clergy have different roles, we share in the ministry of the gospel
  and the priesthood of all believers
- Recovery of baptismal ministry affirms rather than diminishes
  the roles of the ordained in community through the sacraments
  and through the ministry of teaching
- The authority of baptism expansively grounds Christian witness
  in local, cultural, and sociopolitical contexts; the church is mission centered and world centered

- Baptismal principles encourage recognizing, supporting, and sharing authority in community
- Faithful living takes shape in communities where all members—and not just a few (ordained) leaders—struggle to understand and live out the faith
- Living into baptism urges Christians to make a difference in the world; baptismal ecclesiology expresses an intense interest in humanity
- Many of the same lessons about authority gleaned in local communities should inform wider structures
- Availability of the sacraments should not be restricted by the location, size, or income of the congregation
- Recovery of baptismal ministry enables us to look toward a hopeful future

What would the church look like if it took the priesthood of all believers, the ministry of the baptized, seriously? There is no one answer to this question, and yet the research that supports this book suggests that taking baptismal ministry seriously transforms ecclesiology, or our theology of the church, away from inherited models of closed, inward-focused institutions and toward more open and responsive ministering communities. It also suggests that individuals and whole congregations are revitalized and renewed in the process from passive consumers of ministry to communities where the gifts of all are valued and recognized.

We are living in an era where many Christian communities in North America are struggling with financial shortages, declining numbers, and fear for the future. While the renewal of our baptismal callings is not by any means the only possibility or a quick fix, it does offer an alternative vision. In an era when it is so easy to lose sight of the impact the life of Jesus of Nazareth has had on the world for centuries, our capacity to envision possibilities becomes a statement of our faith. *Born of Water, Born of Spirit*, like baptismal living itself, is saturated with responsive hope in God. Hope, as presented in this book, is not a possession or an object. Hope precipitates. It is a living process, a "bold conviction of an alternative possibility," a promise that the present is provisional and open to change.[41] Christians continue to be, as noted in early baptismal

INHERITED ECCLESIOLOGY	BAPTISMAL ECCLESIOLOGY
Closed Eucharist	Open Table
Call as holy orders	Call as baptism
Clergy model	Shared ministry models
"Paid my dues"	Partnership and ownership
Ordained as professionals	Priesthood of all believers
Church's mission	God's mission
Education as information	Education as transformation
Chaplain to needy	Community formed around God
Clergy perform all important tasks	Community members empowered for ministry
Clergy deliver ministry	Clergy developers of ministry
Church meets my needs	Church desires to meet God's needs
Closed groups/guilds	Open/transparent, participatory
Church language	Common tongue/vernacular
Take care of people in church	Nourished people sent out
Father knows best	We all know together/learning
Gathered around a minister	Ministering community
Kingdom after death	Kingdom now
Clericalism	Diverse ministries affirmed
Restricted space	Open and welcome at center
Museum	Interactive and emergent
Hierarchy chooses those educated	Local discernment
Segregation by age	Education for all
Hoarding	Hospitality
Exclusivist worldview	Multireligious and nonreligious world

—Fredrica Harris Thompsett, 2007

testimony from the first letter of Peter, birthed "into a living hope." Daily we are supported in baptismal living not simply by our good intentions but by a God who stands by her adopted children in countless ways. This covenant, like all biblical covenants, evokes a living partnership, an enduring covenant of hope. As Christians we affirm that God's creation of the world is ongoing. So it is with the church. "As long as there are Christians there will be communities of faith—congregations of people gathered for worship and witness in the cities, towns, and crossroads of the world," writes James C. Fenhagen, the author of numerous works on the ministry of the laity. "The question is not *if* but *how*—the question that, by the grace of God, turns us in hope to the future, which is now."[42]

DISCUSSION QUESTIONS

1. Remember your baptism. Whether you recall the actual events or have memories based on others' accounts, what about your baptism is significant to you?
2. This book utilizes the images of "born of water, born of spirit" to focus on baptism and the ministries of the baptized. What images of baptism are prevalent for you?
3. Reflect on your preparation for ministry, both within and outside formal church structures. What are some of the ways the church formed you and supported you for ministry?
4. What are some ways that your own faith community supports members in the ministries of their daily lives? What aspects of human life are embraced by your congregation? What aspects are overlooked?
5. This introduction refers to baptism both in terms of *living hope* and as *sacrament of struggle*. How do you feel these realities point to contemporary baptismal living?

CHAPTER 1

A SAVING REMNANT:
VITALITY IN SMALL
CONGREGATIONS

Some of the smallest congregations in North America are places of subtle vitality and frequent surprises. St. Thomas's Episcopal Church in the village of Winn, Maine, is one such congregation. St. Thomas's has stood on a rise above the Penobscot River for 139 years, its unlocked doors welcoming all those who venture up the hill. Winn was once a bustling town with a hotel, tannery, and railroad station. Now a couple of hundred residents share a post office and a general store. The tiny gothic jewel of St. Thomas's Church draws its membership from an area roughly two thousand square miles, the size of the state of Delaware. Over the course of its ministry the congregation has mothered four other congregations, one of which remains open.

The current congregation of St. Thomas's is now comprised mostly of elders and a half-dozen children. The congregation has wide educational and economic diversity. Some members never finished high school, while some have graduate degrees. Some have traveled throughout the world, while some have never left the state of Maine. Some have steady employment; some have never recovered from the closure of the paper mills. Some have been abused at former faith communities and courageously attend St. Thomas's as they learn to trust again. Most members voluntarily contribute to the congregation's discretionary fund. "At the altar, however, all these differences melt away," says Carolyn W. Metzler, the congregation's vicar at the time of our study. "Then people come forward, kneel (as they are able), and stretch out their open hands."

Despite the challenges, St. Thomas's Episcopal Church is growing deeply in faithfulness. The congregation is steadfast in its ministry in the community, particularly to those most in need. Sometimes this ministry is a community effort, but often it is the individual members themselves who respond to the needs around them, often in quiet, hidden ways. For instance, one of the oldest shut-ins of the congregation gathers stuffed animals and knits mittens for children whose parents come to the food cupboard. A new member donated a bumper crop of squash and a freezer. On another occasion the congregation hosted a benefit supper for the family of a young man in a coma from an accident sustained when falling through the ice. He was not from the area, nor was he a member of the congregation, but the impetus to reach out to his family was there anyway. The congregation maintains a special fund for emergency needs in the area and has given away over a thousand dollars; they give to denominational funds and local charities, and also raised money to fix a water problem in the vicarage. They give to the Heifer Project International and the Episcopal Diocese of Haiti. While these amounts may seem modest to larger congregations, for the people of St. Thomas's, a church in a rural and poor area of Maine, these contributions are a sign of great generosity. With rising fuel costs and bitter winters, the people of St. Thomas's have had to make difficult choices. Many of the congregation's members live on fixed incomes with little to spare, yet they have made a commitment to a $150,000 capital campaign to help secure their financial future.

Carolyn Metzler describes the many signs of vitality in St. Thomas's congregation as "a spirit of reconciliation and hope" that is palpable. Worship remains at the center of the congregation's life, with shared preaching, leading worship, and singing. People claim their mission and seek ministry in their daily lives. In this small congregation, among the thirty-five to fifty worshipers on a typical Sunday, people with a diversity of life circumstances come together at the altar and reach out pastorally when no one has asked them. "And not even my words could give you the sense of how the church smells in the spring or the feel of the darkness in the nave at midnight when the rafters shift and a squirrel runs across the roof. The prayers of 139 years have soaked into the woodwork, blanketing the place in peace," says the former vicar. Carolyn Metzler de-

scribes the congregation's vitality as "generosity breaking out." The smallness of the congregation enables Metzler to know people by their hands
alone, "cupped in front of them and waiting for the holy bread; dimpled,
creased, arthritic, calloused, ringed, bony, pudgy, thumbless, tilted, open,
all waiting expectantly."

Some of the signs of vitality Metzler identifies as characteristic of St.
Thomas's include the following:

- People who struggle financially but still offer their wood leftover
  after winter to someone who needs it more
- Congregation members each taking a week to offer Christian
  education to middle school children
- Although it will cost them, voting as a congregation to embark
  on a risky project to ensure the financial security of the next
  generation
- Offering spontaneously to host a benefit supper for someone
  they don't know, they will never know, and who will never join
  the church
- Not only tolerating children's noises in worship, but also welcoming children in worship
- Worshipers not flinching but expressing compassion when a visitor shouts in loud outbursts during congregational prayers
- Seventeen "old-timers" turning out for the house blessing of a
  new member

Carolyn Metzler says that in 2007 the congregation lost a staggering
eleven members to death, to moving away, and to making other choices.
"We are still a community in grief. When I place the sacred bread into
outstretched hands on Sunday morning, the bread is often baptized with
tears," she says. Although all those who moved away did so for good
reasons, including one couple that had been part of the congregation
for seventy years, the losses are keenly felt. Metzler also admits that it
is difficult not to take the losses personally, or as a comment on her
ministry. Though she believes that the ebb and flow of membership
and Sunday attendance is "a normal rhythm of the spiritual life—people
become involved with other things, take summers off to work in camps

or stay on the lake fishing; if you asked them, they would tell you they are spiritually alive there in the boat or in the woods." Metzler admits that a decline in attendance is a "real trap, however, because there is a subtle assumption that increasing numbers means we are doing well (and therefore I am successful as a priest) and declining numbers mean we are not doing well (and therefore I am doing something wrong). I fight that anxiety all the time. . . . Numbers are terribly seductive idols."

Perhaps because of their small numbers, the people of St. Thomas's have learned ways to reflect on church membership differently. The congregation considers itself much larger than annual denominational statistics suggest when all the categories of members who comprise St. Thomas's are considered. Three distinct communities comprise the congregation: first, the group of people called the "in-house community" who come to worship most weeks, pledge, and are regularly involved. Second is the "out-house community," people who never come on Sundays but have an ongoing association either through special services, educational offerings, burials and baptisms, or outreach. They come through the perpetually unlocked doors to pray in the sanctuary or drop in for a chat. The third is a faithful online community made up of people who log onto the church website, read the sermons, and ask questions. There is no way to know the exact number of these members, although the hidden counter on the website recorded three thousand visits last year, with 16,350 sermon downloads. "The church of today includes all these other people who are also hungry for a word of life and who struggle with their theology, their sins, and their yearning for God," says Metzler.

Although estimates of what constitutes a *small* congregation vary, one common measure among denominations is to consider those with an average Sunday attendance of 100 to 150 or less.[1] Within the Episcopal Church, of which St. Thomas's, Winn, is a part, nearly half (42.2 percent) of all churches can be considered small membership, with 20 percent reporting an average Sunday attendance of fewer than 30 people.[2] Yet public perceptions of vital churches often conjure images of program-size congregations or megachurches. Small congregations are likely to have fewer resources, and consequently they may have more challenges in getting beyond a survival mentality to move toward a theology of abundance and the subsequent recognition of what vitality means in their context.

SIGNS OF VITALITY IN SMALL CONGREGATIONS

A generosity of spirit grounded in a theology of abundance

The sacraments available as desired and not tied to the wealth, geography, or the size of the congregation

Openness to creativity and new experience—new people, new ideas, the arts

Commitment to the ministry of every baptized person—the ministry of every member counts and is received through baptism rather than confirmation or ordination

Extensive and intensive emphasis on hospitality and keeping the doors open to the community; people in the community know to go there for help

Immersion in prayer and worship

Spiritual formation for all is a key value, with an emphasis on small groups for study and nurture

Intergenerational participation in all aspects of community life

Experience of reconciliation and healing of the disjointed parts of members' lives

Shared leadership and decision making at all levels of the community's life

Responsibility for pastoral care, worship, and administration facilitated through shared leadership

A focus on Christ's mission in the world and a commitment to social justice through outreach and service

Ecumenical and interfaith partnerships; celebrates denominational identity in an expansive sense and is open to those beyond traditional boundaries

Ecological consciousness through the care of resources, stewardship, and the environment

If a small and vital congregation were to disappear, it would be missed—not only by its members, but by the wider community as well.

Compiled by Fredrica Harris Thompsett and Sheryl A. Kujawa-Holbrook, Pastoral Excellence Project, Episcopal Divinity School, Cambridge, Mass., 2005

SIGNS OF VITALITY

What does small church vitality look like? To be sure, there is no one definition, and the variations on small church vitality are as numerous as the congregations themselves. Some are located in areas where numerical growth is possible and aggressively seek to expand their membership. Others situated in remote areas where membership growth is unlikely seek abundance in other ways, such as growth in outreach, by extending lavish hospitality to all, or in nurturing the depth of the spiritual commitment of members. In the United States and Canada, many communities have experienced significant out-migration and financial decline due to the departure of industries that traditionally supported the people in the area for generations. For such congregations, the prospects for significant numerical growth are modest or nonexistent, and thus the need to measure vitality and growth in terms other than the strictly numerical is imperative if they hope to respond to the ministry needs of their contexts. Part of the challenge in encouraging vitality in small congregations is to find ways to free small congregations from culturally dictated standards of viability; to free spiritual formation, ministry, and leadership from the prevailing culture of clericalism; and to shape a vision of theological education that is committed to supporting the ministries of the whole people of God.

There is broad consensus among leaders in the small congregations discussed here about factors or characteristics that contribute to small and vital congregations. "Vitality is a quality in response to living into Christ. It may be reflected in quantity, but quality is reflected in involvement in activism, not necessarily parish activities, where members live into actions of compassion, justice, listening, reconciliation," says Anita Schell-Lambert, rector of St. Peter's Church in Bennington, Vermont. "Signs of vitality in a small church which are crucial, necessary, all-important are caring, liveliness, energy, and strength," says Judy Krumm, a member and chair of the discernment committee in the same congregation. A positive sense within the congregation about its ministry has contributed to the growth of the Church of the Good Shepherd in Houlton, Maine, located a few miles from the Canadian border. "Listening to each other is so important," says Leslie Nesin, priest-in-charge. She also suggests that while the congregation struggles financially, the positive spirit within the community makes it easier to close that gap.

More than two hundred people from across the region assisted the congregation of St. Martin's, Palmyra, Maine, after a fire destroyed the church building in April 2006. Lev Sherman, the priest of the congregation, attributes the response to the fire to "the incredible level of involvement" in the larger community of the fifty or so members of the congregation, with an average Sunday attendance of approximately twenty-seven. "If someone in the community gets laid off, or loses a house, we are there to help," he says. Certainly, St. Martin's is important enough to the wider community it serves that it would be missed if the congregation closed its doors. The church building is literally located at a crossroads—the only occupied corner of a four-way intersection. Outreach is a sign of vitality in this small congregation. The congregation made an intentional decision to focus on outreach and less on buildings and grounds. The parish hall, a former Grange hall, houses a computer center, a library, and a literacy program. The congregation also sponsors turkey pie suppers and a county food bank. Funds for outreach are raised by events involving church members as well as people from the wider community. Like many small congregations with outreach efforts, St. Martin's is both gratified by the supportive response of the wider community and challenged to spread its ministries more widely in the face of local needs.

Samuel J. Wylie, the bishop of the Episcopal Diocese of Northern Michigan in the 1970s, suggests that the *norm* in style and size for the Christian life is the small community, and others should take on smallness, or simplicity, as the model. His ecclesiology was based on early Christian, radically equal, Spirit-filled house communities more than current church structures. "A saving remnant was what God used to achieve salvation. And the Savior is assigned a stable instead of a palace and Bethlehem instead of Jerusalem for a birthplace, and Nazareth for a home. . . . *Small,* for many of us, suggests words like puny, mean, isolated. For Jesus it meant the mustard seed that grew to great and expansive measure," he writes.[3] All faith communities are unique, having their own culture and character. At the same time, it is important to recognize the presence of the Holy Spirit in all sorts of congregations, regardless of size, geography, or wealth, calling all members to ministry individually and collectively in their own community and beyond.

Sam Wylie came to Michigan's Upper Peninsula from New York City and soon found his presuppositions about what is important for effective ministry confronted. Wylie realized that our society often takes for granted the idea that bigger is always better, and small is usually assumed to mean either immaturity or atrophy. Although it is hardly guaranteed, he came to see smaller communities as potentially the healthiest and most vital expression of the Christian church. In many cases shared vi-

sion, mobilized resources, common commitment, and change management can happen more easily in small communities than in larger ones.
It is not uncommon to find effective larger congregations that engage
small groups to organize, educate, teach, discern, and support ministry.
The other reality is that in small communities everyone knows each other
and everyone's gifts are needed.

The capacity for vitality in small congregations is a focus in the 2006
study of St. Magnus, a congregation in the Shetland Islands, Scotland,
undertaken by Elaine Cameron. Cameron's work points to the importance of congregation-based theological education models, rather than
those based on individual learning. However global the congregation's
vision might be, it still needs to be grounded in the local community. In
the final analysis, all mission is grounded in the local context. Cameron
says that the people of St. Magnus perceive baptism as the critical fact in
their membership in Christ's body, rather than ordination or confirmation, and thus assume that theological education should be based in the
congregation, not on individual learning. "The curriculum," she notes,
"is both content and process, and it engages head, heart and imagination,
aiming to make connections between faith and life more permeable."
Cameron suggests that the way the congregation perceives its mission
within its context is critical. "St. Magnus has been asking questions about
what they should be doing in a good sequence: For example: *In this place,
what is mission? What ministry does this require? How do we enable maximum
participation? What do we learn in reflecting on the process?* Their confidence
as a congregation grew, so that they began to see that ministry was not
just what the rector did, nor even what they individually did. They began
to see that not only had their congregation a ministry to the world, but
that it also received from the world. Above all, ministry was about what
everyone offered, individually and collectively," said Cameron.[4]

SIGNS OF THE LACK OF VITALITY

For many small congregations, however, unhelpful perceptions about
what a church ought to be and the subsequent feelings of low self-esteem
can seriously impede any meaningful discernment about mission and
ministry. Small congregations often feel diminished when their commu-

nity life is compared to the extensive music programs, graded education programs, and active youth groups of larger congregations.

T. Sammie Wakefield, a member of St. Andrews-in-the-Valley in Tamworth, New Hampshire, who also has experience of small congregations in California, Hawaii, Kentucky, New Mexico, Vermont, and West Texas, suggests that many signs of vitality in small congregations are subtle and in the details. For instance, there are congregations where members seem genuinely happy to see each other and places where the larger community perceives the church as a place to go for help. Wakefield listens for enthusiastic, if not professional, singing, and scans leaflets and bulletins to see signs of life—people involved in different activities and remembered on their birthdays, on anniversaries, and when prayers are especially needed. She believes that a well-loved and cared-for physical plant is an important sign of vitality. "There is a palpable sense of goodness and love in the very woodwork of the physical plant."

Wakefield also suggests five signs that indicate a lack of vitality in a small congregation:

- Policies are not written down so "How we do it" is known to only a few.
- One or two people do everything (closely related to the first sign).
- "Idols" are made of a part of the church; that is, people obsessively focus on things such as an organ, the layout of the sanctuary, or a certain translation of Scripture.
- An undercurrent of troublemaking, such as circulating petitions or secretive behavior, is evident.
- The congregation sees its main function as supporting the physical plant as a sort of historical monument or museum, rather than as a center for ministry and mission.

Many small congregations face the inability to pay for full-time clergy as a trauma and yet another indication that they must decline. As concern for survival sets in, the focus of the congregation shifts inward, and along with this shift is a de-emphasis on the energy, creativity, and commitment likely to attract new members. As the focus of the congregation and leadership base narrows, it is not uncommon for one or two strong personalities with unhealthy and unmet emotional needs to take over, and thus make regaining lost vitality even more difficult for the congregation. Leaders in such congregations must often struggle to balance constant demands and cope with arising crises, with little time for their own personal and spiritual development.

THE SMALLEST SMALL CONGREGATIONS

While small congregations may emulate larger congregations in some ways, the smallest congregations, those with fifty members or less, tend to function differently. In these settings, relationships are of primary importance, and the process for becoming a member often more closely resembles adoption than an educational incorporation process. Leaders with relational strengths are often most effective in these congregations where oral traditions and oral communications are the norm. The congregation's story is often held by elders prominent in the community and particular families play central roles in the story. In these congregations, change happens when the community is ready, and the process needs to consider the whole membership, as opposed to formally designated leaders. In many cases, the congregation includes people with an enormous emotional attachment to the church but who are largely absent from worship life. Although some small congregations struggle with an inwardly focused sense of ministry, there are also examples of small and vital congregations that have a strong sense of mission and ministry beyond their immediate membership.[5]

St. Barnabas, Milby, Quebec, is a small country church with a membership of about twelve families that meets usually three times a year. Here a baptism is cause for another major gathering. Michael Canning, a priest who serves the congregation, remembers that the sanctuary was packed for the last such occasion. "The third generation of this family was being presented at this same church to be watered and anointed into Christ's flock," he says. "Indications are that the family will be invited to participate more fully into the workings of this very small community of twelve families. And so the church carries on being the place where people are constantly reaching out to include, embrace and encourage [other] people to belong."

In 1993 about three people attended weekly services at St. James's Episcopal Mission, Tanana, Alaska. The mission is located on the Yukon River, about 130 miles west of Fairbanks and is only reachable by airplane or, weather permitting, a twelve-hour boat ride. The village of Tanana is a Native American community of approximately 350 people and is steeped in river culture. The Yukon River flows about one hundred feet from the church. Founded by Canadian Anglican missionaries in 1860, the mission is now part of the Episcopal Church and is served by missioner Ginny Doctor and a ministry team. Under Doctor's leadership, the congregation began identifying leaders with the goal of forming a local ministry team. The Diocese of Alaska assisted by providing training to help members develop their skills for ministry. By the year 2000 the community celebrated the ordination of one of its elders. At the same time, more members began to share in the ministry, forming a six-member ministry team of lay and ordained leaders. Other signs of vitality present at this time included the 10 percent the congregation gave away, their efforts to rehabilitate facilities, and the reality that Sunday worship happens with or without clergy leadership. Ginny Doctor says that after every Sunday Eucharist, when she opens the door to look at the river, "Then I wonder, what more will God bring us in our river of ministry?"

Ginny Doctor reports that many good signs of vitality continue to emerge at St. James's, Tanana. The wider community of Tanana (that extends well beyond the village itself) within the last three years raised six thousand dollars to restore a historic bell and stained glass windows reclaimed from an older mission three miles away. St. James also sponsors a gospel and bluegrass music camp for young people. Among the goals for the program is one to train church musicians. Fiddle and guitar are part of the local culture, and the congregation purchased these instruments along with mandolins for young people to use at camp and at home. Ginny Doctor adds that learning music also helps build the self-esteem essential to preventing suicide and drug and alcohol abuse. (Alaska has high youth suicide and drug and alcohol abuse rates.) All the youth events are drug and alcohol free.

By the year 2005, the average Sunday attendance at St. James's, Tanana, grew to twelve members; by 2008 that number had increased to seventeen, although sometimes as many as thirty attend worship. Over half the current members tithe, a big difference in a congregation that once struggled to buy a barrel of oil for heat. Most of the pews have been restored, and the laity and clergy of the congregation share ministry. The people of St. James give readily and generously to local projects and to churches affected by Hurricane Katrina. Ginny Doctor says that part of the growth in the worshiping community is due to the improvement in church music. She learned to play favorite songs on the guitar and made a special attempt to put chords to the hymns the elders favored. "St. James's is truly blessed, small but thriving. Every time that bell rings it is not only a call to worship but a call for one to be thankful for, and remember, all of those in years past whose strength is still present."

As a seminary student, James Pratt was recruited to work as a catechist in the Diocese of Western Newfoundland. At the time the diocese was unable to retain seminary-trained clergy, and the realities of the many small and isolated congregations there made supporting locally ordained clergy difficult as well. Newfoundland is the most economically depressed of Canadian provinces and the hardest hit by the collapse of the fishing industry. There are only a few larger towns. Corner Brook, where the cathedral and synod office are located, has a population of about twenty-five thousand. Overfishing left many of the residents of the small outport villages in the province without jobs or realistic alternatives for economic recovery. While many young people move to other parts of Canada for work, seniors remain in the villages and comprise a large portion of church membership. Most of the small congregations in Western Newfoundland are organized into multipoint parishes. Pratt served in Daniel's Harbour, a parish consisting of three small villages along the west coast of the island, each with its own church. The largest village has approximately 350 residents, of whom 90 percent are nominally Anglican. Visiting the sick is an integral part of the ministry of the church. "Ministry in Newfoundland is truly a cross-cultural experience," says Pratt, "further from my middle-class suburban roots than I ever thought I would get."[6] In spite of the economic need of these communities, he acknowledges the welcoming spirit of these small congregations. "Many times I made pastoral calls I was chastised for waiting at the door rather than just walking right in," says Pratt. "I could never leave without being served a meal, or at least something to eat. As just about everyone stocks their freezer, I learned to like moose, caribou, and snowshoe hare. Fresh baked bread and fresh berries were other treats lavished on me."[7]

Pratt opted to return to Western Newfoundland after seminary and served as the vicar of the parish of Cow Head. St. Alban's, Sally's Cove, Newfoundland, in the Cow Head parish, is situated in a remote village where making do is a way of life. Pratt says that visitors to the congregation notice immediately how welcoming the congregation is, especially when members greet the visitors first, before greeting each other. The people of St. Alban's (of whom fifteen are over age sixty-five) have lost most of the physical signs of their community—school, post office, general store—hence "they strive hard to keep the one sign they have left, their church." In the 1970s, before it was slated for resettlement by Parks Canada (hoping to restore the area to its natural state), Sally's Cove was a village of about three hundred people. Even in the face of possible forced resettlement from their remote outpost to a centrally located commercial center, some residents refused to move. The village now has a population of twenty-two year-round residents, augmented by a few lobstermen who live and fish there during May and June and a few families with vacation cabins. The tenacious core of six "regulars" plus some occasional visitors support the church generously and do all the physical upkeep of the property. Within the past five years, they have embraced shared worship with three other congregations within the parish of Cow Head. James Pratt says that the shared worship is not seen by the congregations "as a step toward merging their congregation out of existence, but as a way of strengthening them by building up the bonds and sharing resources with sister congregations."

One of the strengths of the small congregations in the parish of Cow Head is their strong pastoral ministry program. At present, a team of five lay pastoral visitors, with more in training, conduct monthly visits and are the primary pastoral presence for twenty-five to thirty elderly and shut-in parishioners. Not only has the experience built the sense of community in the parish but it has also been deeply spiritually rewarding to the visitors themselves, who remain in touch with the vicar about pastoral emergencies. Two of the congregations in the parish, St. Mary's Cow Head and St. Peter's, Parson Pond, have started using the adult education and formation resource *LifeCycles* from LeaderResources (see "Resources for Baptismal Ministry," page 179). Most employment in the area is seasonal and many people are hit hard between the time the work stops and when they get their first unemployment check. In response, St. Peter's has organized a local food pantry. Both congregations have increased efforts to broaden participation in worship and plan more special services, such as hanging the greens in Advent and a Lenten devotional service; both congregations have also become more deliberate in bringing friends and neighbors to church.

John Olsson III, who also serves two small congregations in Western Newfoundland, notes the importance of shared leadership throughout the region. "At present, we are in the process of working on a strategic plan for each congregation," he says, "so that folks realize that they do in fact have a say in the creation of their own future, rather than just sitting idly back and letting the future happen to them." Despite the fact that the congregations he serves are small, Olsson reports that they continue to have a significant influence in their area and are seen as important community centers. Hence, members will sacrifice significantly to keep their congregations open and to make contributions to the broader community.

Kevin Cross, who served St. George's congregation in McAdam, New Brunswick, right out of seminary, reports similar challenges and signs of vitality in his congregation. The people of McAdam, a rural town of fifteen hundred, are an independent lot skilled at both self-reliance and care for their neighbor, and characteristic of those who call the community home and who rise to the challenges of the remote location. Originally settled by Loyalists and Acadians, groups that came to New Brunswick rather than be absorbed into new societies, the people there take responsibility for the health of their communities and their churches. With the exception of the Pentecostal churches, the denomination one is born into generally remains the affiliation for life. The average age of the members of St. George's is about seventy and many are homebound. Weekly worship attendance averages forty-five to fifty people per service. The congregation has a small youth group comprised of eight young people with an age span of five to thirteen. Traditions are important, and change, for the most part, occurs slowly. What is considered the ministry of the baptized in some locations is to the people of

St. George's "doing whatever needs to be done." When the congregation was without a resident clergyperson for over a year, worship services continued on a weekly basis, a parish team visited the sick, and
community suppers continued unabated. "The typical lines that we
draw in church polity between clerical and lay responsibility tend to be
blurred," says Kevin Cross, when speaking of St. George's. "Here it is
done as a matter of practicality as well as personal character."[8]

SMALL CONGREGATIONS DO GROW NUMERICALLY

While the sentiment "bigger is always better" does not unilaterally apply to small congregations and their vitality, it is important to note that
there are, in fact, situations where such communities can and do grow
numerically. One such congregation is St. David's Episcopal Church in
Page, Arizona. Page is a tourist town located on the edge of the desert
and near a dam on Lake Powell. The next largest town is about 130 miles
away. Most of the economy depends on the dam, fishing, and boating,
and in the off-season unemployment is high. When Page was founded
in the late 1950s, the government gave land to establish churches. The
result is that twelve churches of different denominations stand in a line
on the main street.

When the new pastor, Steven Keplinger arrived with his wife Jean in
Page in 1999, St. David's was barely open. Six members kept the church
going. Some negative publicity focused on Keplinger's prophetic preaching began to attract some folk to the congregation shortly after he arrived.
Today, St. David's has a membership of approximately 160, mostly due to
the congregation's commitment to take on the hard work of social ministry in a community of great need. "It can be hard to do in a depressed
town," said Keplinger, "but we refuse not to live in abundance anymore.
We will not buy into any scarcity."

Today St. David's is known for its extensive social ministries and
creative worship. The social ministries began with the congregation's
membership "looking outward" and a sense that they could help
"fill the gaps" for the people of the area, says Keplinger. A food pantry was considered the most pressing need in the community, so the
church started one. The congregation's feeding programs now provide

food for fifteen to sixteen hundred people per month in a town of seven thousand. At St. David's, a soup kitchen, counseling center, and financial aid programs have been added to the outreach program that started with the food pantry. This outreach is sustained through the prayer and worship of congregation members. St. David's celebrates its Episcopal identity expansively and reaches out to people beyond traditional denominational boundaries. The congregation created new seasonal liturgies and strives to shape its life of prayer and worship in response to the life of the wider community. "The liturgy speaks to who we are in this place," says Steve Keplinger. "We have got to get beyond studying liturgy and speak to people where they are." Keplinger admits that it is a challenge to plan worship on a regular basis that is creative, innovative, and nurtures people with many different tastes. Like many small congregations, providing a variety of musical styles remains a challenge. Important to note is that St. David's continues to look for ways to grow and to change, including building relationships with the nearby Navajo community.

In 2008 St. David's built a new sanctuary to meet their growth needs. During the building process the congregation met in another church in the middle of the afternoon and compensated for their feeling of homelessness by having more social gatherings and using any excuse to get together as a group in a more intimate space. Liturgies became even more innovative as the congregation worked to capture a sense of togetherness in a strange space. The new sanctuary was designed to recapture the sense of family, even though St. David's has grown far beyond that size category. The social ministries of the congregation did not suffer during the construction; the financial aid offices and the food bank were open the entire time. In 2007 the congregation's food bank was supported by sixty-two volunteers, fed more than five thousand families (approximately twenty-four thousand people), and gave away more than twelve tons of food. The congregation's soup kitchen was supported by sixty-seven volunteers and served nearly thirteen thousand meals, while the Emergency Assistance program served eighty-two families.

Steven Keplinger notes that a next step for St. David's is not to fall into the "our building is finished, let's rest" trap. Instead, parish leaders are looking for new strategies for outreach into the community. Keplinger hopes to grow the numbers of young people in church, to increase the congregation's presence as caretakers of God's creation, and to celebrate the new sanctuary and move forward.

St. Andrew's Episcopal Church, in Colchester, Vermont, a suburb of Burlington, has also significantly grown numerically. Although on the verge of closing several years ago, the congregation's Sunday attendance now hovers near the one hundred mark. The congregation embarked on an intense program of listening and today many signs of vitality are evident as people actively care for each other and the larger community. Keeping a focus on Christ as the center and continuing in prayer and study supports the congregation in its efforts to focus, and not to run in too many directions at once. They focus on worship, spirituality, education, and outreach. Congregational leaders have steadily grown in their sense of the ministry of the baptized; have conversations about stewardship of time, talent, and treasure; and share their faith. A large portion of the congregation is younger families, another group of midlife people, and then a few elders. Congregational leader Mary Lou Ashton, a member of St. Andrew's since 1988, reports that one of the things the congregation promotes with young families "is the idea that the most important ministry they have at this time is taking care of their families and getting them to church." Those who have the time and energy to do more are welcomed, but they are not pressured to volunteer beyond the point where it might be detrimental to their own families.

An ordained pastor and nonordained members of the congregation share leadership in a variety of ministries at St. Andrew's, including a healing group and a grief group. Leadership for the Bible class and adult education is also shared. A welcoming committee works hard to be sure newcomers are incorporated at their own speed over a period of several months. "We also work hard at not overwhelming people with too much attention," says Ashton. Outreach to members of the congregation who are in need, as well as the surrounding community, is also a priority. "We are always trying to raise up new leadership so that some of the people who do a lot can have time off and recreate, and so that newer folk can be incorporated into ministries," notes Ashton. A few years ago the congregation expanded the church nave as well as educational and office space. Membership growth has stretched St. Andrew's financial and administrative needs. The congregation hopes to partner with the diocese in providing ongoing leadership training.

Another vital and growing small congregation in Vermont is St. Peter's Episcopal Church in Bennington. When the current rector, Anita Schell-Lambert, was called to the congregation in 2005, it was obvious that a central concern was the need to engage a new generation of active young people. One of the ways the congregation continues to attract younger members is through music. In 2006 both a children's choir and an alternative worship service, "Sundays at Five," were started. Every effort was made to make Sundays at Five as user friendly as possible, paperless, with as much flexibility as possible, and open to spiritual seekers. "I think it's where we need to be. We welcome everybody from all walks of life," says Schell-Lambert. "We make it so easy to slip in and out." Not only has the use of new music seeped into the other liturgies of the congregation, but also newcomers to the Sundays at Five service almost invariably become "habitators" (frequent attendees, if not members) of the traditional Sunday service at 10 a.m. Schell-Lambert believes that the openness cultivated through new forms of liturgy and music in the congregation has helped the congregation more readily reach out in word and deed to the world. "The synergy between familiar and new, grounding in tradition and ability to try new things, is a model for deepening one's spiritual development, on both a personal and a corporate level," she says. "As with the intentional radical welcome of our first goal, our second goal is causing us to stretch and grow in our spiritual journeys."

"St. Peter's has been very vital to the building up of Bennington," says Judy Krumm, a leader in the congregation and chair of its discernment committee. The congregation has an average Sunday attendance of approximately 140 people over three Sunday services. In a town where the number of churchgoers is technically on the decline, St. Peter's is aggressive in its outreach. The congregation hopes to become a community center and presently hosts various local meetings, recovery groups, and programs for the developmentally disabled.

On Pentecost Sunday, St. Peter's hosted the "Tongues of Fire Chili Cook Off," which brought out local chefs who made fifteen different pans of chili, with prizes going to the top four recipes. The chili competition was part of a series of events celebrating the one hundredth anniversary of the congregation, all focused on the local community. "The events are examples of what the church is doing all around," according to Anita Schell-Lambert. "We want to get as much partnership in building community as we can," she says. "In a culture where people don't automatically go to church, we go out of our way to welcome people. You can't measure the way we do church by the number of people that come on Sunday," says Schell-Lambert. "All these programs we have are not faith things. They are community things. It is not about numbers nor is it about doctrine, it's about helping people. What difference does it make if you have all this doctrine but people are dying in the street?" Other ongoing outreach programs of St. Peter's include an ecology group that started a community garden and hosts dinners featuring locally grown foods. Rector Anita Schell-Lambert also hosts a monthly spot on radio station WBTN in Bennington that focuses on community events.[9]

THE POWER OF HOSPITALITY

Small congregations committed to baptismal ministry, such as those illustrated here, often cite the critical importance of intentional hospitality as key to vitality and ministry to the wider community. Theologian Kortright Davis writes of a "new and surprising spirituality" present in congregations that form community in the midst of intentional social engagement. While many congregations provide some forms of hospitality, Davis distinguishes between efforts that reinforce homogeneity (congregations that focus hospitality on their current members or of those like them) rather than those which truly welcome diversity and advocate the needs of the larger community. Congregations committed to breaking out of patterns that support the status quo are instead called to a communal consciousness based on a sense of what Davis calls "radical hospitality." Rather than seeking out like members for mutual support, congregations built on this more expansive notion of hospitality seek to embrace all, including those people considered beyond the reach of organized religion. Rather than focusing their public theology on outreach programs that maintain the unjust distribution of power and resources in their communities, such congregations see in exercising hospitality a commitment to social justice. Davis believes that this spirit of hospitality seeks to radically change both the individual believer *and* the whole society through a communal vision of social transformation. Davis writes in his book, *Serving with Power*:

> As we seek to discover the true meaning of ministry, and as we struggle with what it means to be powerful servants of the servants of God, we do well to bear in mind that, as faithful Christians, we are all in this search for meaning and this struggle for wholeness together. . . . This requires of us a persistent openness to the leading and urgings of God's good Spirit. These urgings often take us down the paths of a new and surprising spirituality as we discern fresh ways of expressing the age-old faith once delivered to the saints.[10]

Nancy Moore, vicar of three small congregations and pastoral excellence coordinator for the Episcopal Diocese of Maine, developed a hospitality workshop as a way of introducing the ministry of the baptized within the context of community and mission. Moreover, the topic of hospitality addressed a deep need for people in congregations in small communities with diminishing populations. "I arrive with a program teaching them how to make people feel welcome and involved in their congregation; by the time I've left I have seen the lightbulb go on over a number of people's heads," says Moore. "They realize that *they* are ministers of the church, not just the priest or deacon. They have something to offer." Moore says it is particularly gratifying to do the hospitality workshop and receive feedback that suggests how people are claiming their authority as leaders of the congregation and are exploring ways to exercise that authority appropriately.

For example, a couple of participants from a large congregation in Maine attended a hospitality workshop, but six months later expressed their frustration that their pastor was unwilling to try their ideas. After the same pastor had left, news reached Moore that the congregation was using the hospitality practices they picked up at the workshop. "It delighted me to hear that this place with a reputation for being cold and closed off is warming up," says Moore, "and that one of my own congregations reaped the benefit and thought about how we might learn from them. It has come full circle."

While there is no one way to organize small congregations for intentional hospitality, an examination of the efforts of a number of small congregations yields some surprising similarities. In many cases, the commitment to hospitality provides alternative metaphors for living in community and what that means for mission and ministry. Discernment of the ministry for some small congregations has a profound impact on communal identity. In some cases where old spiritual formation models have proved inadequate to support more expanded notions of hospitality, leaders have found ways to support members spiritually through their ministries in everyday life.

HOSPITALITY AND BAPTISMAL LIVING

There is no precise recipe for intentional hospitality in small congregations. Transformation, after all, is a journey, a process for congregational engagement rather than a destination, and unique to each context. However, the following characteristics suggest a congregation's movement toward engagement with an extensive and intentional spirit of hospitality:

1. A clearly formed community identity and commitment to a vision of inclusivity and community outreach

2. Openness to marginalized persons and those not traditionally served by organized religion

3. Worship and ritual that is indigenous and communicates and supports the congregation's mission and identity, while at the same time is flexible enough to allow for guests to fully participate to the degree they choose

4. Spiritual formation and religious education that support individuals of all ages spiritually and in vocation and witness in the world

5. Emergent ministries that are focused on the needs of the wider community and are planned and undertaken in partnership with those served

6. Collaborative leadership willing to take risks and undertake projects with uncertain outcomes

7. Leaders who preach and teach about the integral nature of hospitality for Christian community and who model their commitment to the same

8. A perspective of the congregation as the source of *both* spiritual formation and transformation of its members in the midst of constant change. These congregations see change as an opportunity and new relationships as a gift.

9. The willingness to devote the congregation's gifts and resources—human, money, property—to the mission of the wider community served

10. The ability to reengage and reinterpret ancient truths in the contemporary context; in other words, theology that is emergent and fluid, rather than fixed and static, in an atmosphere that allows for questions and challenge

TRANSFORMATION IN THE CITY—
ONE PERSON AT A TIME

Sara (Sally) Boyles, pastor of Church of the Holy Trinity, Toronto, from 1993 to 2007, defines her role as the animator of the congregation, with a belief in the power of transformation "one person at a time." At a congregation devoted to hospitality in downtown Toronto, Boyles sees her leadership role there as a prophetic one, based in the *process* of transformation, rather than as a minister who holds the congregation together. "I don't feel obligated to mop up the pieces: I hold the observation, not the pieces." Discernment is an important aspect of Boyles's leadership in that she seeks as pastor to focus on where Holy Trinity "is *not* engaged, getting it articulated and setting it loose."

Describing themselves as a "church of inclusivity," the Church of the Holy Trinity of the Anglican Church of Canada orders its life around worship and the arts as well as a commitment to social justice. Although the congregation offers more traditional liturgical fare at an early service, contemporary worship with inclusive language and a diverse roster of laity and clergy preachers is the core of Holy Trinity's principal Sunday service, where the Eucharistic celebration encircles the altar. During the liturgy the gathered community of activists, theologians, tourists, writers, and students are given ample opportunity to share concerns and thanksgivings. Obvious, too, is the congregation's commitment to the wider downtown community through its many ministries, including two downtown apartment buildings, participation in an ecumenical Sanctuary Coalition, and hospice care for the terminally ill. Holy Trinity's longstanding invitation to the gay and lesbian community is also an intentional aspect of congregational life.

Ministry with marginalized people, many of whom have traditionally stood outside the boundaries of organized religion, is not new to the Church of the Holy Trinity; rather, it is an ongoing expression of the intentions of the congregation's founder. Holy Trinity, one of the oldest active congregations in Toronto, was founded in 1846 with a legacy from Mary Lambert Swale, a Yorkshire woman and clergy spouse. She designated the funds for a church with pews "free and unappropriated forever," according to the church website, as a protest against the then-traditional pew rents. The church opened a year later with a diverse congregation of artisans, shopkeepers, Irish laborers, and middle-class families. By the early twentieth century, as the area surrounding Holy Trinity became increasingly nonresidential, parish leaders focused the congregation's strengths in worship and social justice in an effort to attract members. During the 1930s and 1940s the congregation provided food and shelter for people who were unemployed or in the military, while addressing affordable housing and the racist treatment of Japanese Americans. These years also brought the debut of *The Christmas Story,* a moving play the congregation has produced every year since 1937, and ecumenical preaching missions that attracted thousands during the season of Lent alone.

The mission of Holy Trinity through worship and social justice was further expanded during the 1960s and 1970s as laity became involved in all aspects of the congregation's life and governance, including worship. Pews were unbolted from the floor (after years of debate) to allow for a more creative use of space, and guitars, piano, and a cappella singers replaced organ music and the paid choir. The congregation's social agenda grew to include civil rights, feminist issues, gay and lesbian issues, and peace and nonviolence. In 1976, after a protracted legal struggle with urban developers, Holy Trinity won rights to air and light space above and around the church as well as the continuing use of Trinity Square. Today the church continues to use its buildings as a resource for urban mission. Integral to this mission is systemic analysis of the uses and abuses of power within the congregation, the larger church, and the wider community.

While serving Holy Trinity, Sally Boyles saw the need for a balance between the individual and the corporate in Holy Trinity's life. "My primary job [was] to keep enough of a middle to keep the body together." Boyles stressed the need for activists and busy church folk to nurture their inner lives through the regular practices of prayer and meditation in order to prevent burnout. She also worked to maintain relationships with neighbors and with the local diocese. However, she noted, the focus of the congregation suggests that *community* for the Church of the Holy Trinity is more related to the people and needs of the wider community than it is to denominational issues.

VITALITY AND TRANSFORMATION

Anthony B. Robinson in his book *Transforming Congregational Culture* suggests that the purpose of the church today has shifted from the idea of a civic faith to human transformation. That is, our purpose is to change lives. The church is not the saved who then save others but, rather, a community of the followers of Jesus who are in the *process* of transformation, of being born anew through water and the Holy Spirit. Martin Luther said much the same about baptism as an event that takes our whole lives to complete. "A congregation that is engaged in the work of human transformation does not hold a possession that it imparts to others," writes Robinson. "It participates in the ongoing work of God and invites others to share in it. It invites people to share in a healing conversation, in the unfolding work of God for change and renewal of personal lives and all creation. . . . Today, the purpose of the church and its ministries is more adequately described as transforming people in the light of God's grace—revealed in the Exodus, the Incarnation, and the Resurrection."[11]

Willa Goodfellow, a ministry developer who works with small congregations in the Diocese of Iowa, says that her role is essentially "a translator, someone who translates church vocabulary into the ways people live their lives." For instance, Goodfellow tells a story about one small congregation in Iowa that made sets of prayer beads for a soldiers' home, and then extended this ministry to make pink prayer beads for a breast cancer survivors' group at a local hospital. Despite the fact that members of the congregation made and gave away over thirty thousand sets of prayer beads in one year, the ministry team said they had no outreach projects! "Words like *discern* can make people's eyes glaze over," says Goodfellow, "but they can *figure out* what their ministry is in their church. Another congregation developed a ministry project using the new pastor's discretionary fund. Each member of the congregation had the option of receiving ten dollars to fund their passion with the proviso that they return and tell everyone how they spent the money. The results were remarkable and moving: A judge bought soft drinks for a group of prisoners who cleared a park. A physical therapist bought socks for the residents of the nursing home. Children bought food for a food pantry. The process allowed people to recognize the ministries of everyone in the congregation and follow the patterns that evolved, rather than spending a great deal of energy on what they felt they *should* do. The Episcopal Diocese of Iowa is training local ministry teams in seven congregations and hopes the seminary-trained clergy available will serve as resources to the process. Goodfellow likens her role with small congregations to the early Celtic missionary movement. "They knew they were not bringing Christ to anybody," she says, "instead they went out to find him."[12]

Jim Kelsey, the late bishop of the Episcopal Diocese of Northern Michigan, maintained that for small congregations to become vital ministering communities, a transformation in the culture of ministry and leadership must occur. He said,

> Our professional leaders (clergy) need to shift their stance from being ministry deliverers to becoming ministry developers. This is a different job description, and it calls for different gifts than we might be looking for in a charismatic, lone-ranger parish priest, who is the best preacher and liturgist, the most compassionate pastor, the most efficient administrator, the most dynamic youth leader, and the most prophetic community developer, and so forth. Instead we are looking for others who are excited about teaching *others* to preach, to teach, to plan, and to lead worship, to offer mutual care, to use their gifts for ministry at home, in the neighborhood, and the workplace, and within the church community gathered.[13]

Kelsey used the metaphor of a cargo ship, contrasting it with a cruise ship, when speaking of the transformation needed to turn congregations from "communities gathered around a minister to ministering communities." In this vision, noted Kelsey, "We are no longer a cruise ship, where the professional crew serves the passengers as clients. We are now a cargo ship, in which everyone on board has a share in the mission of the vessel. No one is a passenger. Everyone's gifts and experiences are utilized to help accomplish the work we share."[14]

In Northern Michigan, explained Jim Kelsey, for transforming congregations from "consumer-based" religion to "participatory ecclesiology," it is important to take seriously the need to support the ministries of all the baptized. Seminaries, too, need to become centers for ministry development. "Seminaries must not only prepare students for 'small parish ministry,' they must become more skilled in educating their graduates to become ministry developers as a matter of course. Given the number of small congregations in the United States and Canada, graduating seminarians without particular skills suitable for small congregations lack educational integrity." Kelsey described the customary path to ordination in the Episcopal Church, not dissimilar in many ways from other mainline denominations:

> The normal track usually starts with a person's self-identifying, and then trying to convince everyone around her/him that she/he is truly called. [A candidate in the Episcopal Church must be sponsored by a congregation and approved by the bishop.] It takes on a personal campaign flavor, which quickly works its way into the educational process. These people (usually) leave their communities and go to an educational setting elsewhere. After several intensive years of formation, education, socializing, and identity shaping, the person is credentialed and sent off to a new place to "begin ministry." Curiously, that person is eligible to go anywhere—except back to the community that first identified his or her gifts for ministry![15]

In the Diocese of Northern Michigan, theological education ideally occurs in the local community, with as many members as possible participating. Through a covenant group process in local congregations, people are affirmed for various ministries and receive education and training. Locally ordained clergy—priests and deacons—are also part of the covenant group process. After ordination, priests and deacons are part of a local ministry support team, and in no way are they considered in charge of the congregation. A number of the clergy in the diocese who are seminary trained serve as regional ministry developers. The diocese has less than a dozen stipendiary positions, including the bishop and the ministry developers. "As a matter of policy, the Diocese of Northern Michigan is committed to working with communities, rather than individuals, in preparation for local affirmation," said Jim Kelsey.[16]

Leaders in the Diocese of Northern Michigan believe that the time when small congregations should try to imitate large congregations has passed. Too often the result was doing many things poorly. Instead, small congregations seeking vitality need to discern their own calling and their passion and thus do the things they can do well. "These techniques hardly guarantee the transformation we yearn for," said Kelsey, "but we sure do have examples of congregations whose vitality is measured not by their statistical growth, but by growth in the spirit, in vision, in mission, in a common life which nurtures and nourishes them, one and all."[17]

A growing concern among congregations and judicatories in recent years has been to provide training and support to students in traditional seminary programs, as well as those pursuing alternative forms of theological education. Christianne Humphrey, a student at EDS and from Massachusetts, participated in a summer field education experience in ministry development with the Episcopal Diocese of Wyoming in 2007. "Listening to members of the Commission on Ministry speak of their work with locally trained priests and deacons was a great learning experience," says Humphrey. During her second week in Wyoming, Humphrey travelled more than 950 miles on Interstate 80 throughout the southwest corner of the state in an area dedicated to mining, oil, coal, and trona, a hydrated sodium carbonate. Working with an experienced ministry developer, Humphrey also had the chance to visit partnering congregations such as St. Paul's, Evanston, Wyoming, a congregation with a Sunday worship attendance of about forty-five people. Small congregations like St. Paul's do not usually serve as field education placements for many seminaries due to their location and leadership structure as well as their size. The congregation has two locally ordained priests, a locally ordained deacon, and a parish administrator. A team plans worship, and a gifted local musician accompanies a choir of about ten people. Members of St. Paul's work with a diocesan ministry developer who serves as an ongoing resource and as a consultant. But the congregation itself does all the decision making. "Yes and no are not in the ministry developer's vocabulary," says Bruce Caldwell, the diocesan bishop. As is the case with most partnering congregations in Wyoming, the congregation's leadership is unpaid, and typically leaders hold jobs outside of the church. "The purpose of the Diocese of Wyoming is, through shared ministry, to develop vital congregations active in the transformation of the world," says Bruce Caldwell. The five guiding principles that support vital congregations in the Diocese of Wyoming are the following:

- We are called to ministry by our baptism;
- We are a community of equals;
- We are stewards of God's mission, Christ's ministry with the church;
- Organizational diversity makes us strong;
- All that we build must be sustainable.[18]

Steven Croft, missioner and team leader of Fresh Expressions in the Church of England, an organization committed to supporting new ways to form ecclesial communities of the church's life, maintains that the basic building blocks of local congregations should be small groups of Christian people who form transforming communities, not unlike the covenant group process in the Diocese of Northern Michigan. "The concept of the transforming community is offered as a way of catching and articulating that dimension of the church's life which is caught by Jesus's travels with his disciples, by the early Christian house churches, by the monastic communities, by Methodist class meetings, by the house group movement of the 20th century, and by the cell church and base ecclesial community movement of the world Church," he writes.[19] The key to developing transforming communities, according to Croft, is to provide an adaptable, flexible framework that is both open to the life of the Spirit *and* orders ministry in appropriate ways.[20]

FRAMEWORK FOR TRANSFORMING COMMUNITIES

Any framework for transformational communities must

- adapt easily to a variety of social contexts, including small, rural or urban;
- be owned by the local church and wider denomination;
- reflect a clear and shared articulation of theology, mission, and ministry;
- support a mission that is sustainable, given the resources for ministry available;
- have the capacity to give stability to vulnerable communities;
- be open to the call to resource the mission of the whole church to the wider society, including the call to make disciples;
- have the potential for growth.

Adapted from *Transforming Communities: Re-imagining the Church for the 21st Century*, by Steven Croft, published and copyright 2002 by Darton, Longman and Todd Ltd., London.

Strategies for Vitality

One strategy for expanding and sustaining vitality in small congregations is focused on equipping members in several key areas: self-assessment, discernment, local ownership, and congregational development.[21] When available, outside assistance with any of these key areas can be beneficial:

- *Self-assessment* is the process whereby a congregation honestly evaluates its history, resources, strengths, and challenges for ministry. What are the opportunities available to this congregation? What has the congregation learned from its failures?
- *Discernment* is a process of prayerful reflection whereby a congregation reflects spiritually on what God is calling it to as a community. What is the shared vision of the congregation, at this time and in this place? What unrealized gifts and strengths exist in the community?
- *Local ownership* is the process whereby a congregation embraces its shared vision and owns responsibility for living into God's calling. It involves recognizing the power and abundance in its midst. Local ownership also involves a congregation's commitment to participate in the planning necessary to extend its ministry and mission. How can this congregation realize its vision as *the* church in this community? In what ways can the congregation better focus or develop gifts and strengths to achieve its mission?
- *Congregational development* is a process that refers to using a range of available resources to identify, support, and sustain ministry in a congregation. Whether through developing local resources for lifelong spiritual formation or by using formal training and theological education, the emphasis is on equipping all members with skills and support for ministry in the church, in daily life, and in the world. What support systems does this congregation need to realize its calling? How is spiritual formation for all members organized?

Total Ministry

Under the auspices of Total Ministry, the Episcopal Diocese of Northern California has developed processes and curricula to revitalize small congregations, as well as affirm the ministry of each baptized person. The Total Ministry process is both a strategy for action and a mechanism to encourage a widely participatory discernment within the congregation about its mission and ministry. Themes characteristic of the discernment curriculum include servant leadership, baptism, recovering mission, reforming ministry, prayer and the Holy Spirit, making group decisions, congregational dynamics, and gifts for ministry. The goals for Total Ministry within the diocese flow from the theological assumptions of baptismal ministry and support all aspects of congregational life. Each Total Ministry congregation will:

- Build on the best of a congregation's history, respecting its experience in its context
- Be equipped to meet its basic ministry needs from among its members, while enjoying the consultation and support of a Regional Missioner and/or other ministry professional (s), and work interdependently with other congregations of the cluster and the diocese
- Call a ministry team gifted in sharing tasks, committed to strengthening the ministry of all the members, and leading in envisioning opportunities for mission and learning
- Show commitment to lifelong learning and ongoing development, including the calling and incorporating of new members;
- Show other congregations in the diocese the rich possibilities of heeding the call to ministry for all believers and thus revitalizing their congregation's life[22]

The Redwood Episcopal Cluster, one Total Ministry Cluster in the Diocese of Northern California, is comprised of three congregations: Holy Trinity, Ukiah, founded in 1877, and located in the county seat of Mendocino County, with a population of 15,500; St. John's Lakeport, founded in 1899, and located in the county seat of Lake County, with a population of 5,000; and, St. Francis in the Redwoods, Willits, a mission founded in 1978 in a town with a population of 5,000. The preamble to the cluster covenant states the ministry rationale for the relationship between the congregations: "We believe that the stewardship of our life together requires us to develop a model that stresses mission rather than maintenance. Such a model will respect that unique context of each congregation and reveal the gifts of the people God has called together in it. It will enable the baptized to employ their gifts for ministry in both the community and the congregation."[23]

The overall goal of the Redwood Episcopal Cluster is to support Total Ministry development in the congregations as well as facilitate communications and offer mutual support. Included in mutual support and a cluster relationship is a commitment to travel. From Lakeport to Willits is about an hour's drive; Lakeport to Ukiah is about a forty-five-minute drive; and Willits to Ukiah is about a half-hour drive. Getting to any of these congregations involves crossing mountainous ridges, and the roads are usually closed several times in the winter. Governance for the cluster is provided through a coordinating committee of nine, three members from each congregation. Decisions must be ratified by each of the congregations participating in the cluster. The regional missioner works with all three congregations as a resource person, and the cluster has a two-year contract with a ministry developer, funded through the diocese, to help strengthen and expand Total Ministry development within the congregations.

Each of the small congregations in the Redwood Episcopal Cluster has a distinct character, a rich history, and signs of vitality. St. Francis in the Redwoods has gained twelve members in the last three years and is now a congregation of sixty-two active members, with a Sunday attendance of thirty-five to forty. It is one of the first two Total Ministry congregations in the diocese. Most active members are between the ages of fifty and eighty; there are a few children. Willits is on the northern edge of wine country and the southern edge of the redwoods and is home to a diverse community, including old ranching families, back-to-the-land folks, a Hispanic community, and a Native American community. Lumber was once the major industry of the area until all the marketable trees were logged out. More recently, Willits became known as an alternative energy center. Marijuana growing is a source for income for many county residents, which creates challenges for the community.

St. Francis in the Redwoods is a small congregation rich in leadership. Within the Total Ministry model, the congregation has identified for local ordination a priest, ten licensed Eucharistic ministers, three licensed preachers, two worship leaders, and twenty-five people who serve as lectors. The congregation also has two trained spiritual directors, a hospital chaplain, a music minister, and the services of the retired vicar. In 2007 the congregation built the first "green" church in the diocese—a straw bale structure made possible through a substantial donation from a visitor. They are on target in paying for the church's construction, and they also continue to contribute to other causes in the community.

The sense of joy among members of St. Francis in the Redwoods is palpable as they describe who they are and their mission as a congregation. Although members of the congregation are active in many ministries both inside and outside the congregation, all ministries are considered equal and voluntary. "Ministry thus becomes a source of bliss and satisfaction," notes the congregation's profile. "Finding and fulfilling one's baptismal covenant through ministry brings joy, energy, and fulfillment. Nearly everyone in the church has identified ministries, even those who have not been directly involved in the training." The people of St. Francis in the Redwoods work hard at sharing responsibility for their common life. "There is no labeling or blaming. Deficiencies or shortcomings are an occasion for prayer and discernment. The quality of our association is becoming natural and almost unconscious."[24] Despite the vitality of the congregation, members of St. Francis in the Redwoods are also clear about their challenges. Like other Total Ministry congregations they are working on a consistent way to add or replace members, and are on their guard about potential burnout or loss of core ministries. They also hope to embrace more of the community through outreach to seniors and youth. They also hope to strengthen their outreach to the Native American community.

Members of St. John the Baptist Episcopal Church in Lakeport have been working toward establishing a Total Ministry team for about three years. Lake County is a rural community in the coastal range of northern California. Clear Lake, the largest lake in California, is completely ringed by mountains. Many of the people are either government workers or in agriculture or cattle ranching. The wine industry is growing, as is tourism. Lake County boasts 313 days of sunshine a year and is home to a great many recreational activities, including fishing, camping, casinos, golf, and special events. Thirty-five percent of the population of Lake County, the highest rate in California, is over age sixty. Approximately 20 percent of the population lives below the poverty line. Overall, the region is growing due to its affordable housing market.

Most of the sixty-seven active members of St. John the Baptist are older adults. Although small in membership, the vitality in the congregation is evident through the active support and management of two substantial community-wide outreach efforts. St. John's Thrift Shop is open three days a week and makes essential clothing and household items available for a nominal fee to anyone in need—or free of charge to people in dire need. A food pantry is also managed by the congregation, funded through the thrift shop or from donations of food and money from the congregation. The food pantry provides basic food and meals for individuals and families who are in emergency circumstances or who need short-term relief until services from government or relief programs can be accessed. In addition to the thrift shop and food pantry, St. John's opens its commercial kitchen to a community meals program and provides space for Narcotics Anonymous and the Alternatives to Violence court-ordered treatment program. Congregation members enthusiastically support moving forward as a Total Ministry congregation and are "committed to community outreach as an expression of faith." Challenged financially, the congregation hopes for support from the regional missioner in the areas of fund-raising, liturgy, and music and in welcoming a more diverse group of people to the congregation.

The third congregation in the cluster, Holy Trinity Episcopal Church in Ukiah, is proud of their active and award-winning youth group. Ranging in age from six to twenty, the young people of the parish meet monthly and are engaged in a variety of projects, including making bag lunches to be handed out to anyone in need who visits the church. The women of the congregation, through the altar guild and an Episcopal Church Women's group, are active in all aspects of church life, raise money, and "keep things running." Also concerned with outreach, the congregation provides meals for local shelters, as well as space for recovery meetings. The community of Ukiah is a major center for business and culture in northern California with a small-town feel. Its Mediterranean climate supports numerous wineries, pear orchards, and wood products. Key to Holy Trinity's vitality is the congregation's ability to value all its work and faith in the past, carrying that into a commitment to the future.

Josephine "Phina" Borgeson, a deacon and experienced ministry developer who has worked with congregations in Nevada and California, is now engaged in a two-year process with the Redwood Episcopal Cluster. Borgeson has a deep appreciation for the "wonderful, wonderful" people in the three small congregations across a wide geographic area. Borgeson has a unique ability to discern the special gifts of small congregations, as she says, "what they have to build on." "There are no interchangeable congregations," says Borgeson. "The challenge is to find ways to make these congregations sustainable." In the role of ministry developer, she provides different types of help to congregations as needed—continuing education, administrative backup, and prophetic challenge to be connected to the wider world. She finds her educational role most exciting, especially sharing the methods of Appreciative Inquiry and theological reflection. "Small congregations tend to fight fires rather than looking at ongoing reflection," Borgeson says. "I am not a problem person. I prefer to use appreciative methods." Throughout her long experience of the baptismal ministry movement, Borgeson has also experienced challenges. For instance, search processes continue to look for candidates defined by traditional roles as vicars, pastors, and rectors when the skill base needed is really much more attuned to the role of missioners or ministry developers. Also, in some contexts the focus on the ministry of the baptized has become too individualistic, leaving out the need for congregations. Borgeson is concerned that the baptismal ministry movement of thirty to forty years "not lose the vision that created it by keeping the experience, but losing the deeper vision about the transformation of injustice in the world. The vision of baptismal ministry in congregations should really be about these other visions as well."[25]

While all three of the small and vital congregations of the Redwood Episcopal Cluster acknowledge the challenges ahead, the spirit in support of Total Ministry development is strong and has helped the members grow existing ministries, initiate new ministries, and recover their excitement in ministry. As the testimony of "an 83-year-old cradle

Episcopalian, head of an altar guild" suggests about her experience of
Total Ministry:

> I can remember how reluctant I was at the beginning to realize I had to take on
> some of our priest's chores. As an old time Episcopalian, I was used to coming
> to church, sitting, kneeling, taking communion and going home. Now I had to
> take on a bunch of responsibilities, some of which I didn't know anything about.
> I bristled when I heard that we were about to lose our priest and we had to do
> something about it. It seemed to me that was the bishop's problem. But when I
> got the hang of Total Ministry, I found it makes church so much more rewarding
> and interesting to me—to have a role to be responsible for, to feel good about
> taking an active part in keeping the church so inspiring and comforting and so
> much more a part of my life. It's hard to change old mindsets, but it can be done
> and everyone benefits from it. . . . I think that's the secret of Total Ministry—
> people who don't sit back and let someone else do things for them, but who are
> willing to work hard for their faith in God and to spread that faith as far as they
> can through their ministry.[26]

In *Pathway to Renewal: Practical Steps for Congregations*, Daniel P. Smith
and Mary K. Sellon suggest that "A congregation that is truly being
church brings people into a loving, life-giving relationship with God and
others that is transformational."[27] These stories of small and vital congregations indicate people who live in hope, feel deep belonging, affirm
each other in their gifts, and view daily life in the world as the context
for the church's mission. For the people of these faith communities, the
recovery of baptismal ministry provides a renewed calling, purpose, and
direction.

DISCUSSION QUESTIONS

1. When have you experienced your congregation at its most vital?
   When have you experienced generosity that breaks out? What did
   you learn from those experiences?
2. In what ways has your congregation responded to the needs and
   concerns of your community? What is God calling your congregation to be and to do in your community now?

3. How does your congregation support the ministries of all the baptized?

4. Reflect on the "Signs of Vitality" list in this chapter. Beyond numerical measures, what are some signs of vitality in your congregation? From your own experience how would you expand on the list started for you in this chapter?

5. What is the hardest change facing your congregation? What is your role in that change?

CHAPTER 2

BAPTISMAL MINISTRY
AND CONGREGATIONAL
LEADERSHIP

The Border Parish comprises three small congregations—All Saints Anglican Church, Hereford, Quebec, Canada; St. Paul's Episcopal Church, Canaan, Vermont; and St. Stephen's Episcopal Church, Colebrook, New Hampshire—who have prayed and studied together for more than thirty years. Marlyn Neary, the vicar of St. Stephen's Episcopal Church, says that ministry in the remote region has survived "because we have tried to live fully into our baptismal vows." The relationship began in the early twentieth century; none of the churches were able to attract or retain seminary-trained clergy for very long. When a seminary-trained clergyperson could be found, they were often newly ordained and served for only a short time. "I guess you could say that we grew into shared ministry because of benign neglect," says Neary. "But we came to the realization that we all share in the ministry here because we are all ministers." [1]

The organization of the Border Parish now consists of an administrative team of laity and clergy who, Neary says, "pray, study, and do the deeds of Christ in the community." None of the leaders of the Border Parish have formal seminary training; those who are clergy were called out of their congregations and ordained and trained locally. They do benefit from a formal relationship with a seminary-trained clergyperson who serves another congregation and is available to the Border Parish as a resource and for support and encouragement. The congregations have a shared worship schedule, participate in ecumenical programs, and share the hosting of educational and social events. While the Border Parish is based on a baptismal ministry model, it also preserves and affirms the individual identities and strengths of each of the congregations. "You can have sheep and cows in the same pasture and it won't overgraze the field," says Neary.

Although congregations may embrace baptismal ministry for different reasons, most find themselves entering into intentional processes of prayer and study. As members of a congregation discern their gifts and their call, the study of Scripture encourages members of the congregation to hear God's voice as it reaches every aspect of daily life. Through study, prayer, and life in community, the shared nature of God's call to ministry is brought forth in a dynamic vision of the interaction between the church and the world. The congregations rediscover the gospel and Jesus's teaching about ministry and the call of the baptized to work for the restoration of human community and wholeness. Wholeness, or holiness, is fundamental to the call of the baptized. *Holiness*, within a Christian context, goes beyond the notion of good behavior or even of being religious. Rather, it refers to our experience of God, deepened through life in the Christian community, as it moves into the events of our daily lives. James Fenhagen believes that holiness "is not limited to those whose lives are primarily church-centered, but is extended to those whose energies are expended in dealing with the complexities of the world. Holiness is only tangentially related to how active we are in the institutional church—how many committees we serve on, how many conferences we attend, how familiar we are with religious language." Rather, it is related to the "energy and vision we are given as a result of our encounter with the holiness of God."[2]

"Ministry is a function exercised in response to the promptings of the Holy Spirit," notes Fenhagen in his classic work, *Mutual Ministry: New Vitality for the Local Church*. The ministry of the church is always the ministry of the *laos*, the self-conscious journey of the people of God. "It is the mutual ministry of laity and clergy, each supporting and challenging the other in the unique functions they are called upon to perform."[3] Fenhagen offers the following four functions as integral to all Christian ministry:

> *We are storytellers.* In ministry we must be able to articulate and
> *own* the story of our redemption and share it in ways others
> may hear.

We are value bearers. We are sent into the world to bear witness to the gospel and the impact of its message on the whole of human experience.

We are community builders. As the people of Pentecost we are called to be ambassadors of reconciliation throughout human societies.

We are spiritual journeyers. We are people on pilgrimage, always reaching for "holiness" and more authentic ways of living in the world.[4]

The late Marianne Micks, a professor of biblical and historical theology at Virginia Theological Seminary, published works on baptism and the authority for ministry given to those born of water and the Holy Spirit through daily baptismal living, participation in the church, and ministries in the world. "Most of us are looking for a God who is too small and too tame," she writes. "What does this tell us about the power of baptism? The awesome dynamism of God the Spirit should lead us to ask ourselves: with what kind of expectation and anticipation do we prepare for baptism, either our own, or that of someone we love? Do we really expect to be shaken to our foundations? Do we really expect to change? Are we willing to discover that volcanic inferno beneath everydayness? Most often, I suspect we are not."[5]

Micks's theology emphasizes that all those who have been baptized by water and the Holy Spirit are called to ministry "far beyond the walls of any church building. They are Christ's ambassadors to the world. They are agents of the good."[6] Liturgical scholar Daniel B. Stevick writes of baptism in the context of "commissioning for ministry":

> It is not just the redemptive meanings—forgiveness, Christ, Church, the Spirit—that are included in Baptism; it is also the commitments of Christian life. Baptism is—or ought to be understood as being—a commissioning for ministry; it is strength for spiritual combat; it is the ordination of the laity; it is the sacrament of childhood and maturity. It sets one within the people of God, the holy priesthood; it brings one into the Eucharistic fellowship. There is nothing left over that must be said at a later stage because it was not said at Baptism.[7]

Small congregations traditionally underserved by denominations have many leadership challenges. In a similar way, judicatories are challenged to nurture, sustain, and provide education and training across vast geographical distance in areas having limited resources available to meet great human need. In rural, small town, and some underresourced urban areas, the affirmation of the ministry of the baptized within congregations has not only optimized resources but has also revitalized congregations through a renewed sense of their vocation in their communities and in the world. The Anglican Diocese of Auckland, New Zealand, has studied the theology of Roland Allen, an English missionary to China in the early twentieth century, as well as the experiences of the church in Alaska; Nevada; Northern Michigan; Qu'Appelle, Saskatchewan, Canada; and South Africa to address the problem of sustaining local communities to be the church "all the time, not just when an itinerant priest could be present." Baptismal ministry is known there as *local shared ministry*. The following recommendations have been adapted from "Keys to Making a Theological Shift about Ministry," which the diocese offers to other judicatories and local congregations throughout the world:

- Pay attention to the theology that makes the community the unit for ministry, not the individual. Trust the local congregation; God has placed the necessary gifts there.
- Ask the question, how tied to the availability of money for a stipend is the sacramental ministry of the church, your judicatory, or congregation?
- When the ministry of "good pastors" is not arresting the decline in church numbers or the decline in money available for stipendiary ministry, look closely at the ministry delivery model. Consider other options rather than packing up your tents and despairing. Inability to sustain an expensive ministry model does not necessarily imply the death of the church; it might be the first pangs of new birth.
- Assess the maturity of the congregation. What existing ministries of the laity in worship and in daily life in the world are being affirmed and developed by the leaders of the congregation—now?[8]

The recovery of baptismal ministry has moved congregations from traditional, hierarchical, "clergy knows best" models of religious leadership into a way of being that values the gifts of the whole community. Within

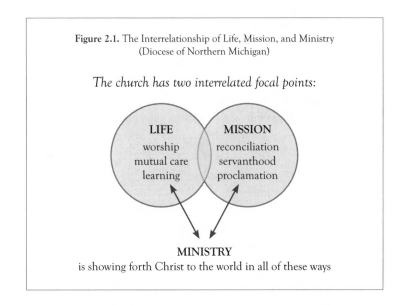

Figure 2.1. The Interrelationship of Life, Mission, and Ministry
(Diocese of Northern Michigan)

The church has two interrelated focal points:

LIFE
worship
mutual care
learning

MISSION
reconciliation
servanthood
proclamation

MINISTRY
is showing forth Christ to the world in all of these ways

this perspective of church ministry and leadership, the life of the church is built around two interrelated focal points: the *life* of the community itself through worship, mutual care, and learning and *mission* through reconciliation, servanthood, and proclamation. *Ministry* is showing forth Christ to the world in all of these ways (fig. 2.1).

BEHAVING, BELONGING, AND BELIEVING

The ministry of the baptized is based in Scripture and the practice of the early church. Although the New Testament contains accounts of instantaneous conversions, most of the earliest Christians, like those of us now, were not exceptional figures like the apostles. In the first few hundred years after Jesus, the ancient Christian community developed a pattern of discipleship that followed the sequence *behaving, belonging,* and *believing.* Rather than starting with the assumption of belief, the making of early Christians centered on the experience of baptism. As Andrew Mc-Gowan, warden of Trinity College, Melbourne, and a historian of early Christianity, writes, "While faith was of course fundamental to being a Christian, it wasn't faith itself that achieved that for you, because the church wasn't quite a voluntary organization in the modern sense, where membership and desire to belong are more or less the same. Rather, baptism was understood to be a transforming action in which God, rather than the convert, was the key player, and in which one actually became a Christian through the action of the Holy Spirit."[9]

In the early Christian world, baptism was considered a radical departure from societal norms and involved costly discipleship that was not ordinarily entered into without a great deal of preparation. By the mid-second century after Christ, an extended period of preparation for baptism, the catechumenate, was developed. Many of the earliest Christian martyrs were catechumens at the time of their arrest, and it appears that the Roman authorities targeted these catechumens during times of persecution. The term *baptism of blood* referred to those who went to their deaths without water baptism, but who nonetheless exhibited a commitment to the Christian faith to the degree that it cost them their lives. The writings of Hippolytus in the third century CE suggest that the catechumenate involved three years of instruction of an ethical nature, less about the actual content of the faith, and that the emphasis was on "behaving," to the extent that a long period of time was needed to allow people to make the lifestyle changes needed to become a Christian. Some people—for instance, magistrates, gladiators, and astrologers—needed to leave their occupations. Catechumens also participated in regular assemblies, where they would receive the laying on of hands and were regularly exorcized. Only after three years of the rigorous catechumenate process were individuals then chosen and set apart to receive baptism. So not until the catechumens demonstrated the ability to live as Christians were they invited into the community (belonging) and allowed to hear the gospel (believing). While it seems that by the fourth century catechumens were allowed to attend the liturgy of the word in the Sunday assembly, they were dismissed before the greeting of peace and the communion. These shifts served to preserve the pattern of full admission to the community only after the baptism itself.[10]

Interesting to note is that on some level, part of the attraction of the early Christian communities to converts, despite the obvious dangers, was the way that the followers of Jesus lived their lives. They were so attractive and morally compelling that individuals risked their relationships, their livelihoods, even their mortal existence to belong. Also, despite the rigorous requirements, the church grew and attracted many who desired admission. As McGowan notes, "The apparent exclusivity of the practice of the catechumenal church is striking. . . . The paradox is that by asserting such clear boundaries but inviting people to negotiate them, the ancient church created a structure which, while not inclusive on a given day, managed over time to appeal to and include more people than our superficially inclusive structures do. Could it be that when inclusion actually means a lack of definition, then we deny those outside the Church something of substance worth coming in for?"[11]

A SHORT HISTORY OF BAPTISM, OR THE TALE OF THE THREE Bs—BEHAVING, BELONGING, BELIEVING

Just because you haven't heard of it, doesn't mean it is new!

In the beginning: The baptized are the keepers of the faith, of the gospel, and members of the Pauline body of Christ. "The people of God" is the most used name for the church.

Second to third century: *Behaving* preceded *Belonging* and *Believing*

Fourth century: Era of institutionalization. Christianity under Constantine ordered as religion of the Roman Empire. *Belonging*, but to whom?

Twelfth century: Baptism a necessary sign of *Belonging* with access to salvation.

Sixteenth century: Reformation; baptism is a sign of *Believing* with many different believers.

Seventeenth century: The New World; at first *Belonging* is most important; among the Puritans *Behaving* is the key.

Eighteenth century: The minister was the preacher. Baptisms and funerals in homes.

Nineteenth century: Development of ministry professionals. *Belonging* most important.

1950 and 1960s: Reaction to World War II. Emphasis in the United States on a learned clergy. European emphasis on lay education.

1970s: Liturgical movement places baptism as the beginning of ministry in the context of *Belonging*. Ministers of the church are laity and clergy (bishops, priests, and deacons for Anglican and Catholic traditions).

1980s: A return to baptismal ministry, also known as mutual ministry, shared ministry, local common ministry. Also a return to the Pauline vision of shared ministry (see chapter 4, "Emergent Perspectives on the Church and Ministry"). *Believing* in the shared ministry of all shaped the *Belonging*.

NOW: A movement again toward *Behaving* by examining the way we behave in the church and in the world. Observed behavior, rather than knowledge of various beliefs, still attracts converts!

—Fredrica Harris Thompsett

MINISTRY ROOTED IN MUTUALITY

Known as *mutual ministry* for more than thirty years, baptismal ministry in the Diocese of Northern Michigan has been concerned with how the "clerically-centered model of congregational life and mission increasingly limits both ministry delivery and the sacramental life of the church."[12] Kevin Thew Forrester, a ministry developer in the diocese, defines baptismal ministry as "a way of talking about how we live in a community of brothers and sisters where leadership is no longer structured around a hierarchy of those of greater or lesser importance, but around the mutual nurturing of the gifts of all members of the community."[13]

Thew Forrester suggests that Jesus proclaimed an alternative kind of community rooted in mutuality and human freedom. A baptismally grounded church is one where ministry is not restricted to the prerogative of the ordained, but one where all members of the congregation have the opportunity to identify their gifts and form them into ministry for the church and the world. Figures 2.2 and 2.3 illustrate the distinctions between traditional models of ministry and the baptismal ministry model. "To be baptized is to become one who accepts the call to serve others. Baptism and ministry are two sides of the same coin. . . . Whether it be preaching, healing, teaching, parenthood, nursing, public service, or the arts, these ministries are the unfolding of our baptismal ministry."[14]

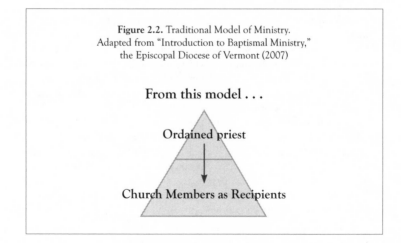

Figure 2.2. Traditional Model of Ministry.
Adapted from "Introduction to Baptismal Ministry,"
the Episcopal Diocese of Vermont (2007)

From this model . . .

Ordained priest

Church Members as Recipients

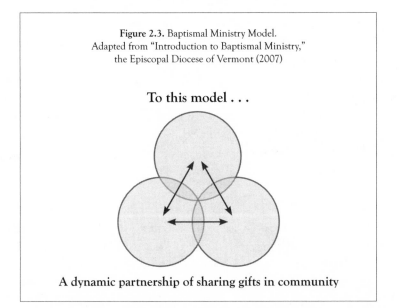

Figure 2.3. Baptismal Ministry Model.
Adapted from "Introduction to Baptismal Ministry,"
the Episcopal Diocese of Vermont (2007)

To this model . . .

A dynamic partnership of sharing gifts in community

Nancy Moore, the coordinator of the Pastoral Excellence Program in central Maine and the vicar of three small congregations there, affirms the impact that a renewed sense of the ministry of the baptized can have on a congregation. "If I was trying to do ministry in a more traditional model, I probably would be overworked and frantic with three churches; but pastoral care could be done here without me," says Moore. "We have people here who really take care of each other. But I then have to let go of the need to know everything and control what is going on." Moore says that in one of the small congregations she serves, her hope is to help people claim "their own authority," the first step of which is to make them aware of it. One of her strategies is to help people make decisions as a group. "The pattern they had 'grown up' with is that the priest or one or two very strong-willed parishioners made all the decisions. People would want to be in leadership so they could be decision makers, but didn't have a sense of cooperation with each other. We have made great strides but occasionally something will come up and I would rather just put my foot down, but overall the congregation is dealing with it." In another of the congregations she serves, Moore notes, the leaders are more skilled at self-governance, "but it was some work when I first arrived to get them to include me in the process. The work in that congregation has also been about making the process more transparent and involving all parties."

As is the case in the Border Parish, Nancy Moore's experience in central Maine suggests that each congregation evolves according to its own
process, and that baptismal ministry moves the congregation to "love one
another so we can love the community," she says. Moore sees her role in
the region as "leader, coach, and spiritual midwife—bringing something
into life that needs life." Baptismal ministry can, at first, "really be a hard
sell," she says, "especially if the people don't believe that ministry is about
them." Moore uses the metaphor of "a new foundation" for the recovery
of baptismal ministry in central Maine:

> Last summer, a parishioner discovered that the foundation of a portion of his
> house was crumbling and needed to be replaced. I watched with fascination
> as the workers placed supports in key places, removed all the old stone, and
> then slowly formed a new foundation in the space left. I have never imagined it
> possible to remove the foundation without the house falling down. . . . [These
> congregations] are finding the "key places" to put some energy and education,
> and slowly deconstructing the old, worn out, ineffective foundation and replac-
> ing it with something stronger and more lasting. The structure may not appear to
> change much, but it will become more stable and safe because of the work done
> on the foundation. We will feel more confident making changes to the structure,
> knowing it's not going to cave in or fall down if we decide to cut a door into what
> was once a solid wall.[15]

Lev Sherman, the vicar of St. Martin's Episcopal Church in Palmyra,
Maine, says that working within a baptismal ministry context means
"shifting toward a theology of abundance." His experience suggests that
the congregation he serves is sometimes adverse to lofty mission statements, rather, "they just do what they do and one of the challenges is
to help them see how what they do is ministry and blessed by God."
Chilton Knudsen, the retired bishop of the Episcopal Diocese of Maine,
believes that some of the best successes the diocese has had in supporting baptismal ministry have to do with awareness of the culture and the
determination to adapt their ministry with and to congregations in light
of that culture. "In settings such as ours, the usual ministerial competencies are not nearly so important as the dogged ability to keep showing
up, and the grace of loving persistently. That is ministerial competency,
indeed . . . the ability to hang out with people, to receive but not react to

the crustiness of northern rural Maine, and to fan the spark which might burst into flame, all that is representative of profound ministry."[16]

The late Wesley Frensdorff, bishop of Nevada, introduced the term *ministering communities* to describe those congregations gathered around the ministries of all the baptized, as opposed to those gathered around and dependent on an ordained minister. Such congregations uphold mutual relationships, where everyone's gifts are valued and where the ministries of all members are supported. Moreover, each faith community is seen as important, with its own unique calling within its context. While there are many local variations, congregations that strive to live as ministering communities share the following characteristics within the wider framework of baptismal ministry:[17]

- Belief that authority for ministry comes with baptism. The baptized share in the priesthood of all believers, yet have different gifts and are called to different ministries
- Belief that the Holy Spirit is active in every Christian community, regardless of size or wealth. God has *already* given the gifts we need to lead the church into the future, if we have the courage to discern our ministries and live into them
- Belief that the sacraments should be regularly available regardless of a congregation's ability to pay for a salaried clergyperson
- Leadership committed to moving away from nostalgia for the past, from unrealistic models of ministry, and focused on God's call in the current context. In every congregation something can be affirmed and celebrated; looking at the future is more energizing if we focus on the life-giving forces present
- Commitment to the exercise of power and authority authenticated by and exercised within mutual relationships. Living in God's wholeness unleashes freedom in community
- Recognition that all ecclesial structures are provisional, and subject to change, as communities and individuals discern their calling
- An orientation both rooted in the history of God's revelation to humankind and focused on the future vision of the reign of God
- Shared responsibility for all aspects of congregational life, including worship, preaching, education, training, outreach, and pastoral care

Wes Frensdorff's theology of ministry widely influenced the baptismal ministry movement and continues to be influential today throughout the world.

BEYOND FINANCIAL MOTIVATIONS

Central Maine is an economically depressed area, and none of the three churches there could support a full-time clergyperson, but Nancy Moore stresses that the growing sense of the ministry of the baptized in the congregation is positive and not simply a response to financial problems. "Economic failure is not a punishment here," says Moore. "The fact that we are doing all that a church should be doing and that we are self-sufficient is something positive." Moore tells a story about an encounter in a local furniture store where she ran into Janet, a member of the Church of the Messiah in Dexter, Maine. The owner of the store knows that Moore is a priest, and asked Janet, "Oh, do you go to her church?" Janet smiled at the owner of the store and replied, "No, she comes to *my* church."

Immanuel Church in Bellows Falls, Vermont, was also renewed through baptismal ministry development. Victor Horvath was ordained an Episcopal priest as part of the congregation's ministry discernment process. Baptismal ministry "gently challenges a church to reframe its own vision of itself and its priorities," he believes.

> In the old model it was fairly easy to subtly pressure people to turn up for some committee or another to "do more for the church." In this model, if we truly believe what we say, we are called to respect an individual's sense of balance and call, and that in turn causes the church to look at its balance and call. Are we willing as a community to let go of aspects of our common life we once held dear (like weeding the garden or making the coffee) in order to support members of the community in answering God's call to spend time with spouses, visit relatives, or read to their children?[18]

Horvath believes that reclaiming the ministry of the baptized in a congregation requires intentional discernment regarding individuals' gifts for ministry and sense of calling. "As individuals, once we recognize life as gift and call, how do we then use those gifts and respond to the call to build and support the community of faith?" he asks.

Immanuel Church is a congregation of approximately fifty members. Although the congregation has an elegant building, like many congregations in former mill towns throughout New England, Immanuel Church experienced a long period of decline. An endowment was left to the congregation in the 1950s, so they had enough money to keep the doors open. But by the 1980s Immanuel Church was a congregation without much sense of shared ministry or identity. Clergy leaders in the early 1990s attempted ministry development, but those modest efforts ceased with the dissolution of that pastoral relationship. Rather than immediately sending replacement clergy, the diocesan bishop challenged the congregation to first discern their own gifts for ministry.[19]

Beginning in 1995 members of Immanuel Church entered into an intensive process that redefined ministry as the calling of all baptized people, in the church and in the world. "I lived the first forty-eight years of my life thinking that ministry was church-stuff," says Victor Horvath. "But what I did at work, or at home, or on weekends came nowhere near to being thought of as ministry. Baptismal ministry as we have talked it and preached it here changed all that in a radical way." A canon pastor was called in 1995 to support the baptismal ministry discernment process. Two years later a group of interested parishioners, called the "map makers group," reflected on the issues of identity, communication, commitment to God, spirituality, and church attendance. During this discernment process, "the time had arrived to be a gathered ministering community rather than a community gathered around a minister." After another year of study and discernment, the map makers both "recognized that 98% of ministry takes place in the world through the activity of every parishioner" and wanted to further explore "what it would be like to affirm and support those with gifts for more church based ministries, such as education, stewardship, diaconate, and priestly ministry."[20] The whole congregation considered the gifts of each member in the vital areas of stewardship ministry, education ministry, ecumenical ministry, preaching, diaconal duties, and priestly functions. Parishwide educational efforts, including newsletter articles, a summer preaching series, and an Advent series were offered. A covenant group was formed comprised of those who responded positively to the invitation for specific ministries and began a three-year period of study. Those called to the ministries of deacon and priest began the diocesan ordination process. On the Eve of Pentecost in 2003, the covenant group was commissioned and ordained as the Ministry Support Team for Immanuel Church, Bellows Falls.[21]

Although baptismal ministry is often linked with financial concerns, Immanuel Church proves that the benefits extend beyond this need. "We come to the understanding of the ministry of all the baptized not out of a need to save money, but because of the simple reason that it is our baptism that calls each of us to ministry," reports Immanuel Church, Bellows Falls. "Money is not an issue for us—the way we carry out Christ's ministry in and to the world is."[22]

The Episcopal Diocese of East Tennessee has been active in the movement to revitalize baptismal ministry, known there as *shared ministry*, since 2003. Rick Govan, ministry development facilitator for the diocese, works with congregations of varying sizes, including those with stipendiary clergy. "We can choose to see this as an opportunity in many of our parishes to be proactive today instead of reactive. From my perspective, if we are truly committed to becoming an empowering church, we must intentionally provide continuity of leadership within our ministries, mobilize members for ministry in a more focused manner, and have mechanisms in place to equip and support each other," says Govan. David Bateman, rector of St. Thaddaeus Episcopal Church in Chattanooga, was somewhat skeptical about shared ministry at first, but grew more interested when he realized that shared ministry was not another new program but a new vision for the church, and one with a proven track record at that. "God is full of surprises. When I allowed myself to get dragged to a meeting 18 months ago with a man I'd never met, little did I dream that our parish might be transformed. . . . And the third impression I had was that we were talking about a way of seeing and doing ministry that was in accord with everything I had been taught in seminary but had always found difficult to implement on my own."[23]

Carter Paden, rector of St. Peter's Episcopal Church, also in Chattanooga, originally thought that shared ministry meant "helping the priest and the parish." However, over time as the congregation grew in its "spirituality and giftedness," so did the sense that "this is not church stuff that is fit in on Sundays, this is about our real life of servanthood."[24] Joani Koch, a member of St. Peter's, is passionate about shared ministry. As someone who has been working with volunteer agencies and churches on and off for twenty years, Koch says she is familiar with every possible excuse about why people do not want to give time to community efforts. The difference with the shared ministry approach is that it begins with discerning people's passions and interests. Only then are they invited to participate in the various ministries of the congregation. "When I call people now," says Koch, "they thank me for calling and are excited about the ministry offered. . . . The new ministry opportunities we have had at St. Peter's have been wonderful because the helpers feel more blessed than helped. . . . I truly believe this is how God created the universe. . . . We human beings are designed to be connected to each other, and using our gifts in this way connects us as the body of Christ."[25]

REDEFINING MINISTRY AND LEADERSHIP

Elaine Cameron of the Scottish Episcopal Church researched "local collaborative ministry," the term the Scottish Episcopal Church uses for baptismal ministry, in the small congregation of St. Magnus in the Shetland Islands. She recently compiled the stories of twenty-one congregations involved in local collaborative ministry in the Scottish Episcopal Church. Cameron says that a key learning throughout the stories is the belief in the "latent potential" released "when people believe that God is indeed calling them. However insignificant they think they are in the world's eyes, God wants them—everyone has their own unique skills and gifts, and excels at something." Most of the twenty-one congregations benefited from gifts discernment, which encouraged as wide participation from members as possible. Cameron notes that members of the congregations also stressed the importance of prayer, Scripture, and silence in discerning their gifts. "Several said that where prayer was the foundation for action, a deeper recognition of God's calling to service that accompanies effective discipleship emerged." Above all, they learned that this way of being church is not an end in itself but a way into fulfilling their calling as the body of Christ. "However global the congregation's vision, members of the congregation emphasized how mission grew out of their local context," says Cameron. "They learned to ask questions in a specific order: 'What is our congregation's *mission* in this time in this place?' before 'what *ministry* is needed to fulfill this mission?' And only then asking 'What *skills or gifts* are required to carry out this ministry? What training or learning do we need?' Mission grows from this local context."

Elaine Cameron says they learned that for a congregation to begin to live into local collaborative ministry takes time "for solid preparatory foundations to be laid through study courses, visits, workshops, liturgy, and so on. It takes time also for people to find their way into what is being explored, and time for 'results' to begin to be seen." Moreover, Cameron found that through the local collaborative ministry process, people learned about themselves. "An important practical discovery was that people liked to be invited to do things, rather than sign up on a list." As members of congregations worked together, their confidence grew, as did their ability to talk about their faith, and their doubts. While this way of being the church is not an easy path, for the congregations in the Scottish Episcopal Church it helped leaders learn the importance of valuing and supporting each other and their gifts for ministry. "They discovered that leaders need to be responsible and accountable, open to fresh approaches to being church, recognizing that there may be value in change," says Cameron. "They need to be in the business of 'permission-giving,' not holding on to power or trying to control." Clergy involved need to be willing to share decision making as well as spiritual guidance with laypeople. Elaine Cameron found great joy in her encounters with congregations who have taken on local collaborative ministry: "Those lay members who are not only embracing the concept of 'being called' and having a place in God's house, but beginning to see that they are also leaders. For all who are called to a place at God's table are leaders there for the world."[26]

Carole Wageman, cochair of the Commission on Ministry in the Episcopal Diocese of Vermont and author of the *Report on Baptismal Ministry in Vermont*, is impressed by the palpable sense of empowerment and interconnectedness evident in the congregation of Immanuel Church, Bellows Falls, and others in the diocese who chose a baptismal ministry model. The personal growth of parishioners who did not see themselves as ministers and "yet are growing into the ministry is a poignant reminder of the gifts lived out in faithfulness by the early Christian church," she writes.[27] Though all congregations are unique, and thus will respond to the ministry of the baptized differently, the Diocese of Vermont has isolated the following five components as integral to developing the ministry of the baptized in a local context:

1. Discerning God's Call—listen prayerfully and reflect together on where God is leading us in our baptismal calling to participate ever more fully in God's reconciling mission to the world in Jesus Christ
2. Self-assessment—honest evaluation of gifts, resources, strengths, limitations, opportunities, and organizational structure
3. Planning—a process of naming clear, shared vision/mission/purpose, setting priorities, clarifying mutual expectations, and naming next steps
4. Local ownership—participation by members in the discovery of gifts and resources to more fully enable the entire local faith community to become what God desires and is calling them to be and do. This leads to a claiming of abundance and an embracing of power that is unleashed by the exercise of mutual responsibility and interdependence
5. Development—ongoing spiritual formation, education, and training using the variety of resources available to identify and develop ministry, establish appropriate structures for mission, and make decisions[28]

Judy Krumm of St. Peter's Episcopal Church in Bennington, Vermont, believes that conversation, cooperation, and collaboration are three elements of infrastructure that assist in building baptismal ministry in congregations. Krumm sees conversation as that which brings people together, face to face, for dialogue and discussion. "In our town, the two-way streets indicate coming and going, and allowing for two directions, two opinions, differences and diversity. . . . Vitality evolves from opportunity for conversations to take place." She views cooperation, another important element for building community, and that which adds much-needed strength to a congregation, "like straw in strong cement. Individual fibers are drawn together, reinforcing the total mass." Further, Krumm believes that building collaboration through townwide projects and abandoning of turf wars creates synergy. "Teamwork and partnerships eventually create more than the sum of the individual parts." The phenomenon of *synergy* allows that the working together of two or more individual people or things can produce a result greater than the individual effects or capabilities. Krumm believes that ministry built on conversation, cooperation, and collaboration ultimately builds community throughout an entire town. "In a small town, we meet in various guises: town meetings, school board meetings, parent groups, music rehearsals, workplaces, grocery stores," she says. "If we have engaged each other in conversation, cooperation, and collaboration about important ethical and spiritual issues, it is much more likely that we will continue dialogue and discussion about political and economic issues. Community is strengthened."

Twenty years ago the seven remaining members of the congregation of St. Thomas's Episcopal Church in Alton, Rhode Island, went to their bishop in anticipation of closing the church. She refused. The small township of Alton is a remnant of a nineteenth-century mill town. The only buildings left in the village are the church and a fire station. The stores, restaurants, and schools are all gone. Yet by 2004 the average Sunday attendance was thirty-one, a fourfold increase, with all age groups represented. Now the people of St. Thomas not only consider themselves a ministering community, they also are said to *depend* on it: "Church is a family, making Eucharist, as Jesus's disciples." For the people of St. Thomas's congregation, the altar extends into their community and includes a soup kitchen, an afterschool program, and the village's first community organization, Alton Community Action.

Key to baptismal ministry at St. Thomas's is its Building Discipleship program, which holds forums every three months designed to help members better uphold their baptismal promises. This program, which began in 2001, is explained as an "ongoing conversation among the members" and occurs for an hour after the Sunday liturgy. The conversations are both constructive and celebratory and focus on three main themes—prayer, mind, and deeds—discussed over a pattern of two cycles: *Prayer*: corporate (liturgy) and personal (ascetic) or spiritual growth; *mind*: learning (catechesis) and social critique (prophecy); *deeds*: caring and administration. The facilitator and the vicar, in consultation with others in the forum, select specific topics. At each forum participants make two or three suggestions for specific action, most of which have now been accomplished. Not only has the program been "deepening and broadening" but also the program has proved to provide a systematic plan for parish administration. Young people choose to participate in the forums as well. Members learned that discipleship "will not just happen, but needs careful planning," and benefits "issue from the regular rhythms of the program (the cycles in succession) more than any single set of tasks accomplished. Habits can help faith."

PRINCIPLES INFORMING BAPTISMAL MINISTRY

- The Baptismal Covenant is fundamental to all ministry.
- Community is always the context for formation, ministry, and mission.
- Mission is the focus of ministry, our response to the call of the gospel.
- The church is ordered to be effective in strengthening the participation of all her members in ministry and mission.
- Every person is called to participate fully in baptismal ministry and life.
- All have been given gifts for ministry, and through baptism, are empowered and authorized to use them in the context of a Christian ministering community or congregation.
- All components of one's life make up one's ministry.
- Every faith community is essentially the base for the spiritual formation and continued encouragement of every member.
- Every baptismal calling in ministry is of full and equal dignity, and each is essential for the fullness of mission,
- The call to specific roles/orders in ministry originates in community rather than from self-selection.
- Effective processes of discernment, formation, education, and preparation for ministry are to be offered for every member of the church, not just those to be ordained.
- Discernment is primarily a process of affirmation of gifts, not screening people out.
- Formation is lifelong, for all, and always takes place in community.
- Vitality in congregations is a sign that God is transforming those faith communities and the wider community of which those congregations are a part.
- The gifts of the Holy Spirit are present in every congregation for the work God desires to be done in and through that faith community.
- Vitality can be sustained by a variety of ministry development strategies.
- Congregational vitality is assessed locally, in partnership with the bishop and the ministry support team, and as strategies for expanding mission and vitality in that congregation.

Developed by the Episcopal Diocese of Vermont. See Carole Wageman, *Report on Baptismal Ministry in Vermont*, 2003, page A26.

BAPTISMAL MINISTRY AND
LEADERSHIP IN LOCAL CONGREGATIONS

Robin Greenwood, provincial ministry officer for the Church in Wales and the author of numerous books on subjects related to the ministry of the baptized, writes that the main task of the local congregation "is to practice community," and thereby "to demonstrate and evoke—however partially—the practice of community in all networks of society."[29] Believing that the church in many contexts no longer has the resources to continue the inherited ministry delivery systems, Greenwood's work looks at how local churches can serve God's mission today by exploring four interrelated theological themes: the image of the *Trinity*, the relatedness of God as three coequal persons living in the freedom of a diverse and authentic community; the image of the *Incarnation*, living as signs of God's body, mind, and heart in the world; the images of *Agents* and *Signs* of the reign of God on earth, acting as agents of justice and reconciliation; and last, the image of *Baptism*, for those who choose and accept it, as that which "confers on all those who are baptized the responsibility for developing their own ministry within the whole mission of the people of God."[30] Greenwood writes:

> Through accepting both resurrection faith and the challenge to wrestle with all that brings down people and creation, we are agents and signs already of what God will have in the end.
>
> The challenge is that as a baptized Christian, I am already commissioned as part of Christ's own ministry. Whether I am ordained or not is immaterial. No matter how I react, the statement remains true. I may be surprised, alarmed, pleased, antagonized, suspicious, acquiescent, scornful or enraged. Nevertheless, by baptism I share in the ministry of Christ.[31]

Jenny Joyce of Mill-Leat Ministries in southern Wales uses the image of an artisan studio and the relationship of master craftsman to apprentice to describe the creative energy unleashed in congregations that recover forms of ministry more inclusive to all members. She reminds us that the term *apprentice* is derived from the Latin *apprehendere*, meaning to seize, to grasp, to learn, or to understand. "Grasping the wisdom of the master-craftsman, as well as the tools of the trade and his working materials, whether of wood, metal, paint or stone, is key to the learning experience," Joyce writes. "He must not only create confidence in the use of his tools, he must also cultivate intuition and working with the nature and integrity of those elements. He must listen, watch and wait. In doing so, he begins to reflect the hallmarks of his Master. He imbibes his master's DNA. If the artist is to remain creative, he/she must forever retain a spirit of *apprehension.*" Translating that model to the church suggests Christ is our master, incarnated in the work of the Christian community, through the work of the Holy Spirit. "Christ is the one through whom we imbibe our DNA. . . . When we share his mind, we share his DNA, and mission spontaneously happens, like an engine spontaneously combusting! We cannot *not* communicate his love!"[32]

Key to the incarnation of baptismal ministry in local congregations is the acknowledgement that in many places church structures can stifle the generosity of the Holy Spirit with a need for order and control. This acknowledgement is in no way a criticism of the many saints and heroes who exercise profound ministries within the church every day, nor is baptismal ministry interested in supplanting those already exercising their ministries faithfully. But it does speak to the realities of many small congregations where diminishing numbers of people face ever-expanding workloads and feelings of frustration as they attempt to continue models of governance similar in many ways to secular business culture, including hierarchical leadership, power through position, authority linked to status, control by multiple communities, and other hallmarks of organizations governed by fear and anxiety. Given these realities, it is no wonder that ministry in general, as well as ministry in small and rural contexts in particular, is considered a killer job with the highest stress levels among professions. The ministry of the baptized, as a recovery of more ancient forms of church governance, is also an opportunity for local congregations, and the church as a whole, to incarnate the life and freedom of the gospel. R. Paul Stevens, who describes himself as a "marketplace ministry mentor," writes:

> The word "clergy" comes from the Greek word "kleros," which means the "appointed or endowed ones." It is used in Scripture not for the leaders of the people but for the whole people. Ironically the church in its constitution is a people without laity in the usual sense of the word, but full of clergy in the true sense of the word—endowed, commissioned and appointed by God to continue

God's own service and mission in the world. So the church does not "have" a minister; it is minister, God's "ministerium." It does not "have" a mission; it is mission. There is one people that reflects the one God who is lover, beloved and love itself—the one who is sender, sent and sending.[33]

The theology of ministry within the Diocese of Northern Michigan works specifically to mend the separation that has evolved between the ministries of laity and clergy, making clergy responsible for the spiritual realm and laity for the temporal realm. This separation has contributed to both clericalism and anticlericalism and has resulted in a second class, often undervalued laity as well as often burned-out, isolated clergy. "In Northern Michigan we try not to use the 'L' word," writes Thomas Ray, retired bishop. "Lay ministry or ministry of the laity invariably means something apologetic, inferior, with low self-esteem. We prefer to speak of 'adult Christian responsibility,' which we expect from each and every one of us as baptized sisters and brothers in the family of Christ."[34]

Within this sacramental perspective, all adult Christians are about making the connections between baptism and life and work. The world is a sacramental place, where all that we can see, hear, taste, smell, and touch conveys the presence of God. The theological challenge within this perspective, for the Diocese of Northern Michigan and other contexts seriously invested in baptismal ministry, is to describe ordered ministry in a way that is neither territorial nor separates the ordained from the larger community. Ray reminds us that the white alb worn by some traditions at the time of ordination represents one's baptismal garment and is not a symbol of separation between clergy and all the baptized. Within this sacramental context, the role of those in ordered ministries is to reveal to us "the depth of mystery of the meaning of baptism," writes Ray. For instance, ordination orders every deacon "to remind us, to reveal to us, to encourage us, to affirm us in that serving ministry that is already deeply embedded in our lives, hallowing our homes, workplaces, neighborhoods, community and church." Similarly, priests are ordered to reveal to us the mystery of baptism by reminding us "that we are a community of reconciliation, a community of sisters and brothers committed to breaking down the artificial barriers that separate and segregate and isolate and dehumanize." Priests do this by helping the community see how reconciling relationships as spouses, teachers, judges, and police officers connect with the community gathered around the Lord's Table so that Jesus, who died to reconcile us with God, can sustain us. The ministry of bishops, apostolic ministry, also is expanded to "shared oversight, education, and witness as sacramentally reaching into daily life for the baptized. . . . For me the breakthrough came when I recognized the awesome, overwhelming, and humbling oversight, not of a diocese, but with my wife Brenda, the shared oversight of parenting: apostolic ministry unrecognized, un-affirmed, and unofficially," writes Ray. "Sacramentally the order of bishop now explodes our awareness and understanding of apostolic ministry into daily ministry that touches our lives at all times and in all places."[35] In other words, the bishop is not a remote, clergy-centered figure but one involved in supporting the ministry of all the baptized.

In the story of the commissioning of the Ministry Support Team of All Saints, Newberry, Michigan, on Super Bowl Sunday several years ago, Ray illustrates how making the connections between baptism, ordination, and daily life can be liberating for everyone:

[All Saints,] Newberry is a congregation with an average attendance of 30 on a Sunday in a space that, if crowded, can seat 60. On Super Bowl Sunday 120 were gathered from the ecumenical community and neighboring Episcopal congregations, with a closed-circuit video cabled into the parish hall. The support team commissioned that day numbered 13, a third of the congregation. Of those thirteen who had prepared together for several years, three were locally ordained priests and one a locally ordained deacon. This congregation can now gather at any time, any day and have a full, lavish, nourishing sacramental life and spirituality. In contrast to the past, they no longer have to await some supply person coming to them from somewhere for them to gather, wrestle with Scripture, offer prayer, and break bread. The members of All Saints remember twenty years ago when they were demoted from a parish to a mission because the local economy had collapsed. They saw themselves as failing, disappointing to themselves, and disappointing to the diocese. Today they share 40 percent of their income with other congregations in their region for seminary-trained support, stand tall, and have this support available at no cost to their budget. Today their sense of confidence and competence and commitment and excitement is life changing. The Ministry Support Team of 13 adults pursued their study and formation collegially, rotating leadership and responsibilities. Throughout the process a seminary-trained consultant companioned them. The team provides support for the daily baptismal ministry of the congregation, but they do not minister to the congregation. This team is not intended to do on the cheap what we previously paid poorly for. That would be reconstituting the old paradigm with poorly prepared volunteers. The locally ordained are not in charge nor is the team. The oversight of the congregation falls to the vestry, which has the support of seminary-trained missioners. Where do the members of All Saints turn for seminary-trained, professional background, seasoning, and support? They have three seminary-trained missioners who are available at any time [through the diocese] for encouragement, information, background, companionship, and assistance. All Saints is a congregation of adult baptized Christians, and they expect serious, professional competence from their missioners as they seek to make the connections between baptismal vows and daily life at home and work, and within their neighborhoods.[36]

Integral to the health of congregations that utilize a baptismal ministry model is ongoing reflecting, connecting, and re-visioning. Part of developing ministry support teams for the long term involves planning regular evaluation and sustenance of the team itself, as well as the other relationships in the congregation. Sustainability of the baptismal ministry model is linked to ongoing cycles of discernment, reflection, and learning fused through the congregation's life and mission.

BAPTISMAL MINISTRY AND JUDICATORY STRUCTURES

Since the mid-1980s, the Episcopal Diocese of Northern Michigan has deliberately created a structure that was shaped by an understanding of baptismal ministry. Before that time, there were congregations that expressed and supported analogous forms of baptismal ministry, but no structure was in place, nor was there a stated theology to nurture and sustain it—and thereby become systemic. Three factors came together within the diocese to set the stage for the current diocesan system of ministry development, one that is now in the forefront of ministry development not only in the United States but also in other parts of the

Anglican Communion and in the world. The first factor was primarily financial: the diocese simply could no longer support the conventional model of one seminary-trained clergyperson per congregation, or even one per several yoked congregations. (The diocese now has six compensated seminary trained clergy and twenty-seven congregations, as well as forty-eight locally trained priests and thirty-eight locally trained deacons.) Another factor to be reckoned with was liturgical renewal, which in Episcopal circles recovered the Eucharist as the primary expression of the community gathered and gave birth to the current Baptismal Covenant. The final factor, as ministry developer Kevin Thew Forrester notes, "was a critical awareness of the debilitating power of a consumer-dominated culture on the church's understanding of community. We had become people gathered around a minister, with the expectation of paying for a divine service. . . . We were convinced that the counter-cultural movement of Jesus invited us into becoming adults gathered into ministering communities."[37]

Thew Forrester draws upon the work of American philosopher Ken Wilber and prefers to speak of the diocesan structure as a "wholarchical community," or "wholes within wholes, embraced and transcended in terms of the scope and field of intentionality, rather than of intrinsic value." He sees the critical issue for all baptismal ministry as being able to account for leadership "while at the same time affirming the giftedness of all." Thew Forrester says that deconstructing more traditional leadership roles based in dominance has been easier in Northern Michigan than constructing new ways of framing leadership within a baptismal ministry context. Jim Kelsey, the late bishop of the Diocese of Northern Michigan, said that they gather their resources within regional structures (sometimes called clusters or area ministries), not to provide a team of professionals to minister to a handful of congregations, but to provide a team of ministry developers who will help congregations assume responsibility for their own life and mission, using shared leadership models. In Northern Michigan these take the form of ministry support teams, and the formation process is called *LifeCycles* (for more information on this curriculum, see "Resources for Baptismal Ministry," page 179). For Kelsey, the heart of baptismal ministry is the shift from "consumer-based to participatory ecclesiology," or shared ministry, and realigning support for the work "from providing ministry from members

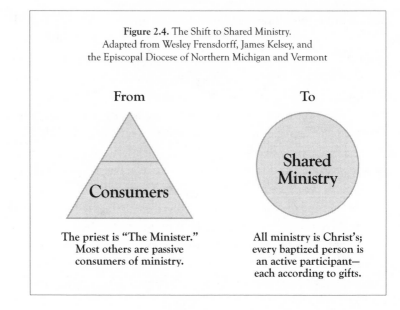

Figure 2.4. The Shift to Shared Ministry.
Adapted from Wesley Frensdorff, James Kelsey, and
the Episcopal Diocese of Northern Michigan and Vermont

From   To

Consumers   Shared Ministry

The priest is "The Minister."   All ministry is Christ's;
Most others are passive   every baptized person is
consumers of ministry.   an active participant—
                           each according to gifts.

of congregations as clients, to having dioceses (in partnership with willing seminaries and other resources and agencies), to become centers of ministry development"[38] (see fig. 2.4).

Baptismal ministry is also a central organizing focus in the Episcopal Diocese of Vermont. The diocese is comprised of many small, rural congregations. The diocese has relatively few full-time clergy; many congregations are served by part-time, bivocational, or locally ordained clergy. Rather than seeing these demographics as a liability, the diocese uses the situation as an opportunity to affirm the ministry of the baptized. "Ministry is the life work of all the people of God. Ministry happens in our gatherings as the church and in the day-to-day living of our lives," says Thomas Clark Ely, diocesan bishop.[39] Ely believes that "baptismal ministry helps take us beyond the realm of the church gathered (as important as that is) and more deeply into the realm of the church dispersed, living out its dynamic discipleship in the marketplace of people's lives—at home, school, work and community involvement." Ely also asserts that congregations striving to live more fully into baptismal ministry are more likely to be focused on mission than maintenance.

Baptismal ministry holds up the primary reason for the church's existence. As one resource from the Diocese of Vermont notes:

Baptism gives every Christian a part in the church's life and mission, a purpose in life, and a new relationship with God and other human beings. Being baptized means we turn our attention to God, believing that God is present in the world around us, that we are in unity with God, and that this unity brings us resurrection. Baptism also admits us to Christ's priesthood. . . . We are a priestly people, and each one of us as baptized members of this people are ministers. If we really believe what we promise in the sacrament of baptism, then all of us stand as ministers in the truest meaning of the word.[40]

During the last several years, the Ministry Support Team of the Diocese of Vermont has continued to refine the way they work with each other, as well as how they see their ministry within the diocese. Diocesan administrators and ministry developers meet intensively for a day each quarter to share worship and a meal, to build community, to learn about the congregations they serve, and to share in professional development. As the circles of communication and shared responsibilities have grown more complex, and as staff is added to the group, the ministry support team is challenged to discuss openly mutual expectations and procedures, while at the same time avoiding the layers of bureaucracy and hierarchy characteristic of many judicatory structures. The quality of the relationships between team members is the key to the inner workings of the diocese's ministry support team. Members commit to intentional relationship building, table fellowship, and a commitment to the team as a form of Christian community. The members of the ministry support team expect both to give and to get support for their ministries from team members, and to share emotional truth candidly and find humor in their work together.

In the last few years within the Diocese of Vermont, and in other judicatories and local congregations engaged in the recovery of baptismal ministry, language has shifted from use of the term *baptismal ministry* to *baptismal living*. The shift is designed to further emphasize that most ministry indeed occurs *outside* of the church, as the baptized live intentionally as Christ's own in the world. The shift in language is the result of concern that in some places the concept of baptismal ministry was limited to including laity in the church's liturgical life. *Baptismal living* is a more comprehensive concept that includes participation in the life of the Christian community through worship, formation, and repentance as well as Christian life in the world through proclamation, service, justice, and peace. Participation in both the Christian community and ministry in the wider world is integral to baptismal living. "In other words," writes Linda L. Grenz, founder and publisher of LeaderResources, "the way we worship on Sundays should embody who we are the rest of the time. . . . It is not a time apart, separate from the rest of life. Rather it is a time that reflects, inspires, nourishes, and empowers us for the rest of life."[41]

BAPTISMAL LIVING AND BAPTISMAL MINISTRY

In baptism believers are transformed into the likeness of Christ to *participate* in God's work in the church and in the world.

BAPTISMAL LIVING
- is carrying out the baptismal promises in everyday life;
- is participating in Christ's work of reconciliation in the world;
- means transforming our communities;
- is incorporating the baptismal covenant into our lives—the *how* and *why* we do what we do.

BAPTISMAL MINISTRY
- is becoming and being a ministering community;
- is participating in Christ's work as done by and in the *local community of faith*;
- is centered in the abundance of the community;
- is a transforming community.

Together, *baptismal living* and *baptismal ministry* are how we participate in God's transformative work in the church and in the world.

Adapted from the Episcopal Diocese of Vermont and the Episcopal Diocese of Northern Michigan, 2009.

Baptismal ministry and leadership is also a central theme in Native Alaskan Episcopal communities. Most of the leadership development for the diocese is done through the diocesan school for ministry, the Father David Salmon School for Ministry. The center sponsors quarterly events on a range of topics focused on the needs of local leaders of Alaska Native communities. Native American elders call most of the local church leaders in bush communities to ministry. Ginny Doctor, of the diocesan staff, says that providing healing for leaders in Alaska Native communities is important. People in the communities experience a great deal of pain around a number of issues, mainly the loss of lands, language, and cultural identities. "The pain manifests through intergenerational posttraumatic stress disorders and is heavy stuff," she says. "But for them to be effective leaders, they have to do healing work." Doctor believes that some of the most important leadership development work the diocese does is through gospel-based discipleship. The many gospel-based discipleship groups throughout the Diocese of Alaska (which comprises the entire state) have become a transformational resource in their communities.

The Diocese of Alaska is in the planning stages of a new young-adult training project, modeled after leadership programs for the age group in the secular world. The Episcopal Academy for Gospel Leadership and Evangelism (EAGLE) will recruit young adults from across the region to join together to form a community of faith and develop leadership skills in areas such as denominational studies, Scripture, church administration, and antiracism. The hope is that the project will help raise up another generation of leaders in small communities across Alaska.

If judicatories (and church leaders in general) are going to retain the trust of small congregations, they need to honor the local culture in which the people live, work, and serve, often for generations. The ministry of the baptized reminds us that the gospel must be enfleshed (incarnate) in the local culture. Louis J. Luzbetak, a cultural anthropologist, writes, "The task of incarnating the gospel in the minds and hearts of the people, in allowing Christ to be born here and now lies principally with the local Christian community—with the people themselves under the guidance of the Holy Spirit in communion with the universal church—and not with the 'outsiders,' however helpful, and indeed necessary, they may be."[42] Lon Oliver, director of Kentucky Appalachian Ministry, believes that "God is always more convincing en-fleshed, and that is what incarnation is about. The Incarnation was not a once upon a time event."[43]

RESISTANCE AND CHALLENGES

Congregations and judicatories that embrace baptismal ministry also face challenges. Despite the benefits of baptismal ministry, many remain resistant to change and suffer from low expectations. Because of turnover of members, the need to develop the ministries within congregations continues. "We have learned that to raise up people from the pew," says Marlyn Neary of the Border Parish, "you have to live here awhile to get a sense of what it [life in the community] is really like. We don't know who the 'third generation' is yet, but we are always on the lookout." Victor Horvath feels that it might be time at Immanuel Church to "reignite that vision of life as blessing and call" among new parishioners who have not yet participated in the ministry discernment process. "So we're reminding ourselves to preach and teach the basics again," said Horvath.

"I have had such a clear vision of the importance of the ministry of all the baptized for so long that I forget that it's a new (and kind of weird) concept to most people," says Nancy Moore in central Maine. "It takes a tremendous amount of energy just to be patient as people discover that I'm not crazy or lazy when I ask them to consider their *own* ministries. It is also a challenge to get people to drive to attend a meeting, training, or even just an opportunity for fellowship with one another." Susan Ohlidal, the pastoral enrichment coordinator for the Diocese of Vermont, experiences the feeling that "we always have to repeat the same message in new ways." Ohlidal sometimes wonders if congregations "are so steeped in the tradition of priest-centered parish life and hierarchical leadership models" that they have difficulty embracing other models.

Chilton Knudsen says that part of the challenge behind doing any ministry in regions like Maine is that congregations are located in very small populations of generally older people who live with multiple stressors: few social or medical services, poor housing, economic difficulty, physical isolation, and sometimes complex family issues. Isolation tends to foster a suspicion of outsiders. "Hard lives feed a cynicism that is not so much hostile as it is resigned," she says. "This means that the sheer challenge of doing their lives takes, for many people, almost every bit of energy that they have. But Maine is, to my great joy and our great blessing and opportunity, profoundly *interpersonal* and *relational*. If folks know you and trust you, because you have just showed up a lot without bringing a big agenda, they will begin to take off the earmuffs which prevent their hearing anything new or different."

Knudsen believes that key to breaking down resistance is "building trust so that creativity can flow." Her theological perspective is that when it comes to challenging contexts, the best strategy is to build a "ministry of presence, which is ultimately about incarnation, God's presence with us in Jesus, who shared our entire human reality, including our limitations." For Knudsen, the image she nurtures about baptismal ministry is about Jesus calling us friends, "and our answering the call to be friends with one another. In this context of being friends (built on many hours of shared life), we can move forward."

Garret Keizer, a locally ordained Episcopal priest in Vermont, wrote *A Dresser of Sycamore Trees: The Finding of a Ministry*, a candid spiritual memoir of his experience of ministry in the small community of Island Pond in Vermont's Northeast Kingdom. As a young man he struggled with discerning his vocation and wondered if he was called to a life of ministry, teaching, or writing. As his call unfolds it appears that his vocation includes all these ministries. Keizer earned a living as a high school English teacher and now is a full-time writer. The title of the book comes from Amos 7:14 where the prophet is called from his work as a herdsman and "a dresser of sycamore trees" to preach. Keizer says that originally he never considered ordination, but he was approached by the bishop only months before the book's publication and was eventually ordained as a local priest to serve that community. "I would be dishonest not to say that I have sometimes wondered if I ought to have remained a lay minister," he writes. "In some ways I feel that I had too short a time to explore that vocation. Ordination has brought with it an increased sense of my own inadequacy, at times almost a sense of displacement. Of course, this may mean no more than that serving as a priest has heightened the awareness of my own human condition, quite irrespective of my ecclesiastical condition."[44]

By his own admission, Keizer has grown in his sense that as a locally ordained priest he became "more reliant than ever on a gathering of friends, each no less 'a dresser of sycamore trees' than I am. And some, much more so."[45] Keizer writes that since *A Dresser of Sycamore Trees* was published he has received many positive responses to the concept of local ordination. Yet his personal response is more mixed, although he readily admits to the joys of local ordination. "It's not that I have any great love for the institution of a professional priesthood. It's rather that I have come to believe that having lay people do what priests do is never so important as having lay people do what lay people do," he writes.

> Much of the true "work of the church" takes place outside of the church build-
> ing, at the job site, in the legislature, and not least of all in the household. (Ecol-
> ogy and equality, not less than charity, begin at home.) One purpose of sacra-
> ments is to make us see that. One purpose of the priesthood is to assist us in
> celebrating that. . . . The church is also the tomb where we go each Sunday to
> find the grave clothes of our Beloved, and to hear yet again the words: "He is
> not here (at least not so preeminently as you suppose). He is risen and goes to
> Galilee before you." We meet Christ on the road. Of course, it helps if you can
> recognize the one you're going to meet. Hence the angel at the tomb, hence the
> service at the church.[46]

Thomas Ray of Northern Michigan has seen that taking baptism seriously is life changing, yet to uncover and recover the paradigm if baptismal living is challenging for all. "Clergy may have to struggle with an
identity crisis as I am, but be assured, the adult baptized (the laity) will
remember when all that was expected of them was that they congregate
around the minister, tithe, and appear respectful. God is taking us into a
future where giving 10 percent of whatever would be a piece of cake. God
is seeking all that we have and all that we are. And that commitment is
what we have truly always sought and yearned for."[47]

Baptismal ministry also challenges theological education. It suggests
the need for educational models that address the issue of accessibility
in order to reach a wider audience than traditional and expensive residential seminaries do. Congregations interested in exploring baptismal
ministry often cite the need for more education and training. If existing
theological schools took the ministry of the baptized seriously, theological education would be more grounded in congregational life, culturally
diverse, and widespread among both laity and clergy. Within the framework of baptismal ministry and leadership, theological education should
not be an elite resource, hoarded or parceled out among the few. Neither
should only those congregations who can afford clergy salaries have access to the ministries of the word and sacraments. There is a deep need
within all sorts of congregations for more ministers who hold up, represent, and remind us all of the priesthood of all God's people.

B. Edmon Martin and Lance R. Barker suggest the following attributes for theological education inclusive of the ministries of the whole
people of God, all the baptized. Such a theological education stems from
the real life of congregations:

- A theological education grounded in the practices of the ministries of local congregations
- A theological education concerned for the development of ministering communities, rather than the development of the individual theological professional
- A theological education accessible to all who yearn to deepen their faith understanding and discipleship
- A theological education in which the whole church is freed to be in the service of Christ[48]

One example of theological education rooted in the ministry of the baptized is the Co-creating Ministry Program (CMP) of Mill-Leat Ministries in southern Wales. The program uses experiential learning to equip all people, churchgoing or not and regardless of educational background or potential ordination status, in service and ministry. CMP and other such programs centered in baptismal ministry intentionally move away from inherited patterns of theological education. Instead they aim to prepare people for leadership in congregations, or not, and for a more holistic way of life, as well as provide a learning experience that supports them in their vocational journey. "Vocation is the response to inspiration, not to a system," writes Stewart Zabriskie. "Vocation is then our acceptance of the Spirit's coordination of our gifts, and the Spirit provides the energy, the momentum, and the context to live out the promise and to extend the center in whatever arenas may be offered."[49] Chapter 3 includes a more in-depth discussion of models of ministry development.

CONGREGATIONS AS LEARNING COMMUNITIES

Inspired by the Great Commission (Matt. 28:16–20), Gary and Kim Shockley, in *Imagining Church: Seeing Hope in a World of Change*, suggest that "*making* disciples is the foundational work of the congregation."[50] One of the key characteristics of congregations seriously engaged in baptismal ministry is the commitment to a vision of a learning community that is intentional about spiritual formation for people of all ages. "We need to move to a radically different way of forming Christians—a way that results in people living a radically different way of life, a life transformed by Christ," writes Linda L. Grenz in her book *Transforming Disciples:*

We live in a world that is increasingly fragmented, with families spread out across the country and with people moving and traveling frequently. In this environment, congregations need to be intentional about building relationships. Small groups, fellowship times, mentoring, and encouraging members of our congregations to spend time together are all ways to build relationships, especially small groups that are focused on doing a ministry or learning together.[51]

The ability to embrace and support gifts for ministry is linked to developing the capacity of a congregation as a learning community. A learning community is more than a Sunday school program or a Bible study or an adult forum, as worthwhile as those activities are. Identifying gifts for leadership is an educational task as well as an organizational one. The act of leading involves individuals, teams, and whole congregations making decisions, solving problems, planning for the future, examining the Christian tradition, all processes that contain inherent educational opportunities. When this happens, church leaders have moved beyond facilitating social and psychological processes. They are shaping and reshaping meaning in a community of faithful practice.[52] Thus congregations and judicatories that take the ministry of the baptized seriously strive also to be learning communities, creating continuous opportunities for education and engagement, promoting inquiry and dialogue, encouraging collaboration and team building, and empowering members toward a shared vision.

Rather than utilizing more traditional "schooling" models of Christian education, ill-suited to the culture and resources of small congregations, the concept of *learning community* suggests that all are teachers and learners, and groups form to learn from each other. While learning communities may choose to use outside resource people, such as a ministry developer, the decisions about the educational agenda remain with the congregation. The learning community model, similar to the model of base Christian communities, is a shift from the reliance on a single authority who orders knowledge, with students as the receivers of knowledge, to a form of shared educational leadership where the assumption is that everyone in the group has authoritative knowledge to share. In the learning community model, leaders more frequently act as group facilitators, or animators, who evoke the insights and reflections already present in the group. It takes reflective practice for congregations to develop the group skills and relationships needed to become real learning communities. Learning communities not only focus on providing people with religious information; they are also intent on helping people *reflect* on what they have learned and *apply* that learning to baptismal living. Baptismal ministry support teams that operate in congregations and on the judicatory levels are one example of intentional learning communities. In the baptismal ministry support team, members discern their ministries, learn, worship, and are ordained and commissioned together as they support the ministries of the congregation. "If we are to be Christ-bearers—reconcilers who carry out Christ's ministry of reconciliation—then we need to act in ways that are reconciling," writes Linda L. Grenz. "Just talking about it—learning all the scripture passages and theological terms, becoming proficient in dialoging about all of the various 'issues' of the day—are all for naught if we cannot empower Christians to act as Christians."[53]

Grenz suggests these characteristics of learning communities:

- Distributed control
- Commitment to generating and sharing new knowledge
- Flexible and negotiable learning activities
- Autonomous community members
- High levels of dialogue, interaction, and collaboration
- A shared goal, problem, or project that brings a common focus and incentive to work together

Over time, Grenz observes, learning communities also tend to develop the following characteristics:

- Capacity to adapt to local conditions and evolve over time
- Creativity and innovation
- Crossing of traditional disciplinary and conceptual boundaries
- Appreciation of diversity, multiple perspectives, and epistemic issues
- Community members who are responsible and skilled at diagnosing and addressing their learning needs[54]

Often it is easier for small congregations to rely on outside experts rather than to take ownership for formation processes for all ages. Yet congregations who do persevere experience a transformation from inherited models of Christian education as *program* to a renewed sense of the need for *ongoing formation* as normative, as the responsibility of the whole community, and as integral to baptismal living and ministry. As Jim Kitchens, co-pastor of Davis Community Church, Davis, California, writes:

> The Spirit is inviting us to re-envision how we will bring people to faith under the more comprehensive rubric of Christian formation. Such a re-envisioning will broaden our imagination and deepen our practices of enculturating new Christians. We will begin to think of worship, small group ministries, and engagement in mission—as well as more traditional educational programs—as formative processes, shaping new and old converts alike so that they grow to reflect the life of Christ more clearly in their own lives.[55]

Transforming Leadership

The experience of congregations and judicatories that have engaged the joys and challenges raised through a recovery of the ministry of the baptized also begs the question about the nature of transforming leadership. "And only where the guides and leaders of the churches are themselves trustworthy and stake their lives on what they do will 'people of God' follow them," writes Anton Houtepen, professor of ecumenical theology and missiology at the University of Utrecht. "That is why it must be said that the church must constantly be reborn. Unless the 'people of God' allow themselves to be incorporated into God's living building as living stones, there will be no temple, no view from any prospect, no place to which we can look to find God."[56]

If in fact as the people of God, the baptized, we are called to transform the church and the world, what then are the characteristics of transforming leaders? How do the gifts and skills needed in the church today compare to those taught in theological schools? "The call to the theological formation of the *laos* is more than a call to teaching new skills and educational programs under the old paradigm," writes Eleazar S. Fernandez of the World Council of Churches. "It is not simply providing lay training on the many 'how-to s;' it is not simply a call to a new responsibility. Much deeper and more radical, it is a call to a new sensibility, to a new way of thinking, dwelling, deciding and acting. In short, it is a call to a new paradigm."[57]

Leadership theorists and organizational development thinkers today have written about chaos theory, signaling what they see as a paradigm shift to an assumption that the world is relatively *unstable* with intermittent periods of reliability, from the opposite assumption of stability as the norm. All sorts of organizations, including churches, are asking questions about the degree of governance required and how to balance the need for order with an equally strong need for creativity and risk taking. The time-honored strategies and organizational patterns of church life in the past are not necessarily helpful any more. While many church leaders have long doubted the veracity of the response, "*But, we have always done it that way before*," chaos theory suggests that what we did before probably is not relevant anymore. "Sometime tradition seems frozen under a great ice shell but below this frozen and rigid surface flow fresh springtime waters," writes theologian Elisabeth Behr-Sigel. "It is up to us, with the help of God's grace, to break the ice that is above all the ice should our hearts become cold. . . . From the ancient spring we will drink water that will give us a new force so as to answer the questions of today."[58] For small congregations and judicatories, the recovery of the ministry of the baptized has proven to be an ancient spring and a source of revitalization in the face of the challenges to ministry presented by the world today.

The first to use the term *transformational leadership*, James V. Downton, a sociologist of leadership and new religious movements, wrote about characteristics of transforming leadership:

> Transforming leadership . . . occurs when one or more persons engage with others in such a way that leaders and followers raise one another to higher levels of motivation and morality. Their purposes, which might have started out as separate but related, as in the case of transactional leadership, become fused. Power bases are linked not as counterweights but as mutual support for common purpose. Various names are used for such leadership: elevating, mobilizing, inspiring, exalting, uplifting, exhorting. The relationship can be moralistic, of course. But transforming leadership ultimately becomes moral in that it raises the level of human conduct and ethical aspiration of the whole organization, and thus it has a transforming effect on both.[59]

Downton's exploration in leadership suggests several characteristics of transforming leaders that relate directly to leaders interested in furthering the mission of small congregations and judicatories today. It is important to note when considering these characteristics that transforming leadership is an organic *process*, a way of life such as baptismal living, rather than a formal course of study. Over time the transforming leaders learn to *inhabit* their ministries, as the boundaries between life and work grow more porous and merge. Transforming leadership is a pilgrimage, a worldview, a gospel commitment, and a chosen way of situating oneself in the church and the world. Some of the characteristics of this pilgrimage follow, adapted to church contexts. Keep in mind that transforming leadership is organic, and therefore listing them is not meant to suggest that the characteristics are ranked or sequential.

INSPIRING A SHARED VISION

Transforming leaders paint an imaginary picture of the community's potential future and share it with others, encouraging them to make it their own and listening as others also shape the vision. When the vision is elevated to the level of the common good, all in the community raise one another to higher levels of motivation and morality. Characteristics of shared vision include the ability to provide meaning, to inspire and excite, to inspire individuals to extra effort, to create a common sense of community, to discern the vision within a group, and to view change as opportunity and promise.

MODELING THE WAY

To be effective, vision must be shared with everyone in the community through repeated communication. The transforming leader must clearly and repeatedly articulate the shared vision. The vision is clarified and enriched through stories, analogies, symbols, ceremonies, rituals, and traditions. Inspirational appeals are effective in persuading people of the importance of the vision. Transforming leaders give life to the gospel by living the vision.

ENABLING OTHERS TO ACT

Transforming leaders are approachable, humble, friendly, and informal. Teamwork is one of the highest values of a transforming leader. They are sincere in their invitation to engage in meaningful dialogue and two-way communication. These leaders frequently act as mentors, coaches, and teachers to those with whom they share the vision. They emphasize recognition for others, both formal and informal. They encourage social functions and educational enrichment opportunities. All of these actions contribute to developing trust within the community.

Encouraging the Heart

For a community to thrive, a supportive environment must be cultivated. Transforming leaders do this by treating people of diverse backgrounds with respect, distributing justice, correcting injustice, and acting with unfailing honesty and integrity. This is accomplished with clear communication and is institutionalized when others in the community respond in the same way with others. Transforming leaders value what their hearts, as well as their heads, contribute to any given circumstance.

Challenging the Process

Transforming leaders shape the community through their own actions and by personally guiding the implementation of the shared vision. They do this through educational enrichment, team building, strategic planning, innovating, and setting high expectations with continuous quality improvement. They embrace opportunities to do things better and take sensible risks to improve the community.

Inhabiting (Incarnating) Their Role

Transforming leaders exhibit character of the highest order, demonstrating honesty, integrity, and unquestioned nobility of heart and mind. They exude passion, commitment, and native intelligence. While they have many characteristics in common with charismatic leaders, they use their leadership to advance the shared vision of community rather than to attract followers for their own sake. These leaders have a broad perspective that they demonstrate with a high degree of tolerance for ambiguity, a healthy respect for history, and attention to issues of cultural sensitivity.

Achieving Results

Transforming leaders achieve shared vision. Those with whom they share the vision are moved to highest levels of satisfaction. All in the community are mutually perceived as having expanded their mission and effectiveness.

"The 'great transformation' exists only in germ in each of us. Its frui-
tion lies ahead," writes Marianne Micks of baptism. "That insight is a
healthy corrective to any theology that sees baptism as an instant or over-
night accomplishment, for baptism is the starting point of a process."[60]
Congregations and judicatories exploring baptismal ministry need time
to reflect on the implications of transforming leadership for all. In many
cases, even where the church community is sensitive to the tendency to
displace the responsibility onto clergy, there remains a tendency in congregations to form a group or groups of ministering individuals, rather
than form a true ministering community. Attention to the process of
ministry development in a congregation and to the collective capacity
for discernment is critical to building ministering communities. William
Stringfellow, the late Episcopal layman, lawyer, and social activist, writes
about discernment as one of the most important gifts for baptismal ministry in community:

> The powers of discernment are held by Saint Paul to be the most necessary to the
> receipt and effectual use of the many other charismatic gifts (1 Cor. 12). Discern-
> ment furnishes the context for other tasks and functions of the people of God.
> . . . Moreover, discernment represents the fulfillment of the promise of Jesus to
> his disciples that they would receive authority *and* capability by the Holy Spirit to
> address and to serve all humanity (John 15:18–26). . . . And discernment is there-
> after always evident in practice wherever the Church is alive (Acts 2:12–21).[61]

BAPTISMAL MINISTRY,
TRANSFORMING VISION, AND THE CHURCH

The belief in *metanoia*, God's capacity to enact deep change in individuals and communities, lies at the heart of the Christian faith. In many different regions and communities across the world, Christians are choosing to collaborate in the ministry and mission of the church in a deep
way, reflecting an intentional partnership between all the baptized, laity
and clergy alike. This vision of ministry and leadership suggests that the
ministries of laity and clergy are inextricably linked within the ministry
of the whole baptized community. Each member of the community, as

part of the body of Christ, through the gifts they are given, is a source of mutual empowerment to the others. Because models of clergy-driven ministry run deep in many congregations, adopting an intentional focus on supporting the ministry of all the baptized requires an intentional long-term process. One ministry developer estimates that it takes a congregation or judicatory at least seven years to make the paradigm shift from a clergy-driven entity to a "ministering community."[62]

Supporting local leaders in more effective ministries makes practical sense in these times when church finances are stretched and where it is increasingly difficult to provide full-time stipendiary clergy for many congregations. However, the positive impact of taking seriously the ministry of the baptized, the priesthood of all believers, should not be limited to financial benefits. Rather, the recovery of baptismal ministry opens up the possibility for the transformation of the whole people of God, and thus the Christian church, in new and exciting ways.

DISCUSSION QUESTIONS

1. What is the story of your baptism? What does the story tell you about the role of baptism in community? How have your ideas about baptism evolved over time?

2. In your own experience, is believing, belonging, or behaving the most important emphasis in baptism?

3. What image or metaphor best describes leadership in your congregation? Try to select an image or metaphor that opens up possibilities for the future. Where are opportunities in your congregation that point toward future leadership?

4. What are the gifts you have to offer the church? How might you use these gifts to make a positive difference? What skills or training would assist you as a leader?

5. How do you experience your own sense of calling? Where do you feel most fully alive? When do you feel most in touch with your power and authority as a baptized Christian?

6. What stories or passages in Scripture point toward your experience of your own leadership in the church?

CHAPTER 3

DEVELOPED, NOT DELIVERED: LOCAL MINISTRY DEVELOPMENT

W hat do small vital congregations in the Episcopal Diocese of Wyoming, a landlocked state that spans 98,000 square miles, and congregations located in the Scottish Episcopal Church, a territory surrounded by ocean on three sides encompassing 30,400 square miles, have in common? More than one might think. Their everyday approaches to local mission, their theological assumptions about leadership, and most of all their ways of identifying, educating, and supporting ministry are cut from the same baptismal cloth. Leaders in these two locations have each learned from a third judicatory, the Episcopal Diocese of Northern Michigan, located on Michigan's Upper Peninsula. Together these three settings represent a movement that is evident to date in congregations across the United States, as well as churches in Canada, the United Kingdom, and New Zealand. Although the denominational setting for these stories is primarily Episcopal, leaders in other denominations are beginning to take note of these ministry development strategies for adaptation in their own contexts, especially as they seek to build vitality in small congregations.

The language used to describe this organization of mission and ministry is generally known as *ministry development*, or *local ministry development*, terms that describe a structure for supporting the development of the ministry of the baptized. The major transition for congregations is from dependence on imported professional ministers to reliance on a community where ministry is typically locally provided and shared by most, if not all, members. Early on, in the history of this movement, this shift was described by Wesley Frensdorff as moving from a community "gathered around a minister" to a "ministering community."[1] It is helpful to think of this model of congregational development as moving from ministry *delivered* by paid professionals to ministry *developed* from the ground up, largely by local inhabitants. Lest we suggest that ministry development is either inexpensive or unprofessional, it is important from the start to acknowledge the dedicated, energetic, and strategically different ways that judicatory officials fund, promote, and seek to sustain congregational vitality through ministry development.

To support this practice of congregational development at the local level, judicatory leaders assign ministry developers to identify, educate, and support ministry in the local context. Some of these ministers work in clusters, some serve as judicatory resource staff, some are pastors of congregations located in or near a fertile mission field. These people are clergy and lay ministry professionals. They carry different titles in different settings; in addition to being called ministry developers, some are known as regional missioners or vicars, ministry enablers, or development officers. The mission they support is also variously referred to as mutual ministry, baptismal ministry, local common ministry, and total ministry. What they have in common is a job description that is significantly different from that of a full-time pastor assigned to be the person in charge of one or more parishes. The Living Stones Partnership, a consultation of more than twenty-five judicatory, diocesan, and institutional partners involved in ministry development in North America, has for the past fifteen years gathered annually to share ideas and learn from one another. Several members of Living Stones have developed with other partners competency statements for the professional vocation of a ministry developer.[3]

This chapter will discuss various ways congregations and judicatories are committed to recovering the ministry of the baptized through forming, training, and commissioning local leaders for work in the church and in the world. Attention will be paid to education and spiritual formation within local congregations and to education for alternative paths to ordination. We will describe the general competencies for those who now serve, or seek to serve, as ministry developers. In addition to stories of success and vitality, this alternative to traditional models of professional leadership has raised questions, challenges, and, in some instances, out-right resistance. Apparent limitations may also be discerned within this relatively new movement. Since there are few geographic regions where structures of ministry development are the only developmental option for congregations, it is important from the start to acknowledge the predominant reality of a mixed allocation of congregational leadership where traditional and emerging models of ministry development exist side by side.

Setting a Table in the Wilderness

More than thirty years ago when a new bishop, Thomas Ray, arrived in Northern Michigan he discovered to his surprise that the traditional sys-tem of clergy leadership—assigning one priest to one parish or even to a cluster of parishes—was neither thriving nor realistic. Many congregations on the Upper Peninsula were not open year round. There were both full- and part-time clergy; some of them served more than one small congrega-tion. Most clergy were geographically isolated from one another. They and the populace as a whole faced shrinking financial and demographic resources in an increasingly depressed economy. Clergy, often trained in seminary to be "in charge" of a medium- to large-sized local congrega-tion, typically did not stay long. The immediate challenge, as Tom Ray would later name it, was how to "set a table in the wilderness." How could he help secure the administration of sacraments and the health of each congregation?[4] Clear to Tom was that importing clergy to serve in the traditional model was not the answer. Tom and others gradually developed a plan to encourage ministry of the baptized in the life and mission of congregations. They called this model "mutual ministry." This strategy was deliberately designed so that everyone's gift, voice, and opinion would be valued.[5] In this developmental plan, as the judicatory now states publicly, "all ministry is Christ's; every baptized person is an active participant therein, each according to gift; and the main ministry is in the midst of daily life."[6] Northern Michigan's approach strives for the spiritual transformation of both individuals and their congregations through personal storytelling, personal skills development, assessment of strengths, and alignment of church systems.[7] They describe this process as an "integral approach" to ministry development. (See fig. 3.1.)

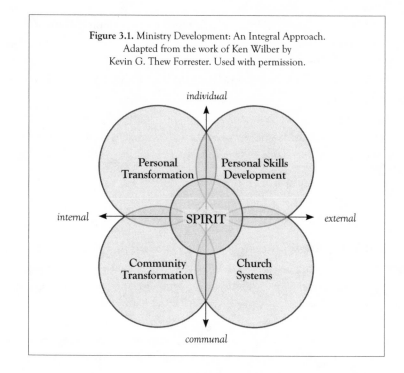

Figure 3.1. Ministry Development: An Integral Approach.
Adapted from the work of Ken Wilber by
Kevin G. Thew Forrester. Used with permission.

When leaders in Northern Michigan decided to pursue the strategy of mutual ministry they were drawing upon the experiences of more than thirty years of missionary work with small congregations in Alaska, Nevada, and other rural areas primarily in the western half of the United States. They were also inspired by the writings of Roland Allen, an English missionary to China at the end of the nineteenth century. Biblically grounded in Pauline ecclesiology, Allen's originating vision emphasized that congregations already had spiritually inspired gifts that would allow them to thrive as self-supporting communities.[8] Today Roland Allen is again being discovered by church planters and emerging church advocates. More of his transformative vision is discussed in chapter 4.

Three other elements were in place by the time Tom Ray was advocating what he often called a "radical reformation" toward ministry development for the Upper Peninsula.[9] The first was a change in governance that allowed clergy to be locally educated and ordained for service in specific remote or isolated situations. The second, and by far the most important

theologically for the long term, was a series of revisions in the denomination's central book of worship, the 1979 *Book of Common Prayer*. This
prayer book recognizes in its catechism that all ministry is grounded in
baptism. It also speaks of laypeople as "ministers" who are to "take their
place in the life, worship, and governance of the church."[10] Shared or
mutual ministry is one way to live out this rhetorical statement. Another
resource, which had anticipated the exciting and exacting changes about
to occur in Northern Michigan, was homegrown. Samuel J. Wylie, one
of Tom Ray's predecessors, authored *The Celebration of Smallness* in 1973.
This pamphlet advocated, theologically and biblically, a ministry of abundance, shared presence, and mutual responsibility in small congregations.[11] This farsighted text remains a prophetic resource for those today
who work with small member congregations. Wylie died in 1974 shortly
after this pamphlet was written. Yet three decades after his death, most
congregations in Northern Michigan embrace his vision and celebrate
the abundant gifts of shared ministry in small congregations.

MINISTRY DEVELOPMENT

A RELATIONAL PROCESS
- Congregation explores baptismal ministry supported by judicatory
- Ministry developer assigned to work with congregation
- Congregation as a whole involved in prayer and educational discovery
- Formation and education of covenant group ministries within congregation
- Cooperative evaluation of covenant group by judicatory
- Judicatory commissioning and celebration of a congregation's ministry sup-
  port team
- Ongoing development of ministry continues in congregation and judicatory
- The process is intentionally begun with succeeding generations

KEY FACTORS
- Ministry development builds and deepens *relational partnership* between a
  congregation and judicatory
- The overall process depends on intentional and ongoing prayer, study, and
  formation
- Ministry development, as a change strategy, involves a multiyear commitment to the process, and then the cycle needs to be continued to integrate
  future generations

Compiled and adapted from documents from the dioceses of Northern Michigan, Vermont, Oregon, and Maine

Mutual ministry, as it came to be practiced in Northern Michigan, involves a transformation of both consciousness and church structures. This transformation takes time as well as ongoing commitment from the judicatory. The process of forming mutual ministry teams typically involves congregational and judicatory leaders in nonhierarchical partnerships based on building deep, trustworthy relationships, and on sharing power.

In Northern Michigan the overall process is grounded on building trustworthy relationships at the local level. With support from the judicatory, a congregation agrees, often initially for financial reasons, to explore the possibility of mutual ministry in their life and mission. Then, a seminary-trained, and often an ordained, regional ministry developer is assigned to be the consultant for that congregation throughout the process. The ministry developer may occasionally provide sacramental care, yet his or her primary responsibility is developing ministry within the congregation. Congregations first participate in a prayerful *discovery process* in which they explore and deepen their understanding of the ministry of the baptized among other foci. A *covenant group* is next formed of those who have initially been discerned for designated roles, depending upon the gifts and mission needed for each community. Roles may focus on such aspects as music ministry, children's ministries, outreach projects, and ecumenical and interfaith relations. The size of the covenant group varies; a general invitation is issued to others in the wider faith community who might wish to join. Then, educational resources are shared widely so that the congregation itself becomes a learning community. Covenant group members agree to study, learn, and pray together regularly for two to three years. The ministry developer serves as a consultant providing resources for the group, rather than being the person in charge. During this period of preparation, members of the congregation, who in many instances have known one another for decades, come to identify and affirm one another's gifts for ministry. This practice of theological education and formation builds trust and deepens relationships within the congregation. The ministry developer and other judicatory leaders lend their support and assistance throughout this period.

The covenant group culminates, usually after three years of locally based formation and education, in a public commissioning of a *ministry support team.* On the team are those who have been identified as having the gifts to support ministry in that local setting: some may be ordained as local deacons or presbyters and priests, others to ministries of music, outreach, education, hospitality, preaching, ecumenism, and so on. In Northern Michigan, ministry is not defined as lay versus ordained. Fostering the ministry of the baptized is the central intent. The central objective of the team is not to *deliver* ministry but to *support* the ministry of everyone in the congregation. Apparently this goal is not unrealistic. One congregational member noted that they have very few PSAs, which she defined as "pew-sitting adults." Everyone is welcome to join in ministry, and most members do. When the congregation discerns a need to refresh its ministry support team, a new generation of covenant group members will be convened to study and pray together, and will eventually be commissioned. Ongoing learning continues to be a central component of the ministry support team, with the ministry developer serving as a resource person for the group.[12]

Trinity Church in Gladstone, Michigan, has followed this process for more than twenty-five years. This congregation is located on the northern bay of Lake Michigan. Gladstone is a small town with a population of under five thousand and twelve churches besides Trinity. In the 1970s Trinity Church had fewer than ten members. Today the average Sunday attendance is fifty with a list of eighty-five active members. Trinity is a thriving example of ministry development at work.[13] Mutual ministry at Trinity Church begins and thrives in all ages and stages of relationships. Five-year-old Benjamin Flaminio proudly shows a visitor his baptismal certificate, signed on the day of his baptism by *all* members of the congregation. Emphatically in the baptismal service and in print, all members of Trinity Church agree to support Benjamin in his life in Christ. This large, impressive certificate takes the place of a small card that in traditional parishes is signed only by clergy and a few designated sponsors. Benjamin introduces one signatory, Helene Merki, now a centenarian, who has been Trinity's organist since 1955. Helene, sometimes called "Mother Church," rejoices in children who are "our best recruiters."[14] Although it took some getting used to, Helene recounts with delight how the church began to grow and thrive with mutual ministry from the 1980s onward.

Sue Ray was identified first to be a deacon and later, in another covenant group, she was called to be a local priest. She still praises the experience of formation that allowed her to get to know people in an entirely different way—people she had literally known for years. On weekdays, Sue is a nurse and administrator in a long-term care facility. She, like others, speaks of this as her "everyday ministry or daily ministry." Her participation in the ministry support team is her "Sunday ministry." Emphasis on ministry in daily living is not neglected. Trinity's ministry support team, which describes itself as functioning as a "group of equals," includes several commissioned preachers; catechists; worship, education, music, and ecumenical coordinators; as well as priests and deacons. Trinity Church is now undertaking its fourth generation covenant group.

This whole new way of being a prayerful, participatory congregation has resulted in lively and collegial worship. Members step forward to assist with a task whenever the need arises. They are pleased with the opportunity to hear the several different preachers identified and trained in this parish, and enriched by the variety of voices and experiences. Trinity still benefits from a warm and ongoing supportive relationship with Rayford Ray, its ministry developer. Ray, who from time to time may be found sitting in the congregation, also serves as regional ministry developer with five other congregations in the region.

There are financial and relational advantages for Trinity Church and other mutual ministry congregations in Northern Michigan. Currently, all but a handful of Northern Michigan's congregations are involved in various aspects of mutual ministry. Four regional ministry developers are assigned to be supportive consultants. For this regional ministry a congregation pays 40 percent of its net disposable income to the judicatory, plus an overall assessment of about 21 percent. In total this amounts to far less than a congregation would have paid for a full-time clergyperson. Remaining funds are spent on building maintenance and church activities with 10 percent regularly given to outreach. Trinity Church, as with most other mutual ministry parishes, emphasizes outreach and justice and peace issues. Whenever possible the congregation donates to local charities. In addition, most mutual ministry parishes are involved in specific volunteer activities in the community. Trinity Church has a long record of being engaged with local schools. Early on, this parish started a "reading buddies program" and an afterschool homework program; both programs have attracted involvement from the wider community. While limited finances were a factor in Trinity's entry into mutual ministry, what is now unmistakable is the vitality and life within this congregation. Local priest Carol Clark speaks of the pervasive sense of joy as well as appreciation that "nobody has to do it all." New goals are being met, including physical improvements for accessibility. New generations of ministry support team members are emerging through covenant groups. And as one member freely boasted, "If we were given three million dollars, we would not go back to the old model." Mutual ministry has given Trinity Church new life.

Northern Michigan's model of mutual ministry development has attracted many others. The late Jim Kelsey, Tom Ray's successor as bishop, was zealously effective in advancing mutual ministry in the region and spreading the good news about ministry development throughout the wider church. So many inquiries came to Kelsey's small judicatory office, staffed primarily by himself and a secretary, that he and the regional missioners decided to advertise and hold annual visitors' weekends. Visitors and locals could participate in lively conversations about the strengths and challenges of ministry development, enjoy warm hospitality, and visit local congregations. Guests seeking new directions for encouraging mutual ministry in their own congregations came from near and far—from Africa, Australia, Canada, New Zealand, the United Kingdom, and places throughout the United States.

On Michigan's Upper Peninsula, with its limited resources in terms of jobs, industry, and future prospects for younger generations, both finances and recruiting new leadership are of concern. Following Jim Kelsey's sudden death, judicatory leaders decided to build upon their familiarity with ministry development in seeking their next bishop. A group representing various regions and leadership has been established to lead the search process. Their year of concentrated time together in study, prayer, and personal storytelling led to discernment of the needs of the diocese and the position description and the qualifications for a new bishop. One of the conclusions that they came to was that no one person could meet expectations or would have all the gifts of apostolic leadership, much in the same way no one ordained person would possess all the gifts needed for leading a congregation. To date they have decided that the single leader model would not be healthy for a new bishop or for the diocese as a whole. They plan to position the new bishop within the con-text of an Episcopal Ministry Support Team. Team members, including the new bishop, would be grounded in a local community serving as a regional missioner. They hope by this process to build a team of equals in which each team member's unique gifts are honored and the burdens and joys of ministry are shared and discovered together. The role of this judicatory team is not "to do ministry" but to support the mission and ministry of all the baptized.[15] As experienced ministry developer Manuel Padilla concludes, the central question that baptismal ministry and min-istry developers attempt to answer is "How do we form our members to be an effective Christian witness in the world?"[16]

LEARNING IN PLACE

Scotland and Wyoming are two regions that have participated in the Diocese of Northern Michigan's visitors' weekends, learning from them, from New Zealand, and other locations in North America. Each region has made ministry development indigenous in slightly different ways. Variations in ministry development are worth noting, as they underscore a significant undergirding of this movement: the importance of the lo-cal setting and the value of building deep relationships in that place. Indeed, one of the mottos of the ministry development movement could be borrowed from the world of commercial real estate: "location, loca-tion, location."

A briefing paper from the Scottish Episcopal Church on "the impor-tance of place" emphasizes the value of congregations rooted in their local context. Such beneficial characteristics as stability, heterogeneous solidarity, local sustainability, and the value of smallness emerge in congregational narratives. Articulating and striving for these goals un-derscores the sense of worth and significance congregations are able to experience in their own locale.[17] Faced with losing viability in many rural congregations and presence in many communities, church leaders wisely observed over a decade ago that "systems constructed for one age do not fit another." Scottish leaders conceived a pattern of ministry develop-ment. They called their model "local collaborative ministry (LCM)." The development of LCM congregations is one path judicatory leaders have chosen to respond to the need for radical change in the structure of rural ministry. Today more than forty congregations are involved in various ways with local collaborative ministry.

Anne Tomlinson, who from 2002 to 2008 coordinated work with LCM congregations for the Scottish Episcopal Church, shaped with imagination and collegial support a plan grounded in providing theological education and skills training. Anne's youthful experience of lessons learned in a base ecclesial community in Bolivia would prove formative. Tomlinson remembered the significant comment of one woman in rural Bolivia: "We are all theologians here." Principles of partnership in teacher-learner relationships, of mutual respect, and of Bible study that directly informs faith in daily life now directly shape local collaborative ministry in Scotland. The emphasis upon entering into congregational formation is offering theological education and skills training for all. As Tomlinson notes, "In a book entitled, *The Rise of Professionalism*, Magali Larson has commented that 'education is now the main legitimator of social inequality in industrial capitalism.' Similarly, the way in which *theological* education, deliberately or otherwise, had been handled by the Church has made it, likewise, the main legitimator of *ecclesial* inequality."[18]

Tomlinson describes the institutional church as emerging from "a clerical paradigm" of theological education. She insists that everyone who wishes ought to have access to educational resources and skills training. Values of educational access and affordability are familiar in Scotland. Most ordination training, for example, is competency based and delivered through courses offered in residential weekends, at regional centers, and in a short summer-school session.[19] Similarly, educational resources provided to LCM congregations are user friendly and locally delivered.

Local collaborative ministry provides the educational framework for a new way of being the church. In its most complete implementation it involves restructuring a congregation so that it can participate as fully as possible in mission and ministry. The pathway for LCM congregations moves in three phases. The journey begins with educational materials and conversations focused on inquiry into their baptismal responsibilities. It then moves on to an exploration stage where each community's strategies, needs, and gifts for mission are discerned. Some congregations, at a later stage when they are more confident, may advance to drawing up covenants with locally identified leadership teams.

This framework depends throughout upon useful educational materials and trained mentors. Resource materials and workbooks, produced by Tomlinson and other judicatory leaders, have been described as both elegant and useful. A 2008 evaluation of LCM made clear that these resources are widely appreciated and regularly put to work. Three modules, *Laying the Foundations, Listening to the Context,* and *Making the Connections,* put forward flexible introductory materials that can be easily used by those in the local community. The why, what, who, and how of ministry are explored with careful attention to the local setting. There are also handbooks on listening and visiting skills, group work skills, preaching, and shaping vital governing vestries. A foundational resource, *Journey of the Baptised,* focuses on a variety of ways for the local congregation to recognize itself as the primary locus for mission. A significant feature of these materials is that they focus on both mobilizing for mission and gathering for worship. Whether assembled in gathered communities or scattered in the world, LCM congregations strive to be alert to their baptismal responsibilities.

In addition to the primary goal of creating congregations as learning communities, a focus on mission is critical for LCM congregations. As Robin Greenwood, author of several books on reimagining the local church asserts, "The Church of God then, does not have a mission, but the God of mission has a church."[20] As part of a minority denomination in a country with an established church, each LCM congregation is asked to discern its local mission. This process takes time, often a year or more of learning, prayer, and Bible study. They explore pertinent questions: What is the mission of the church in *this* place? What ministry does that mission require? And how do we enable as many people as possible to participate to the maximum of their potential in the church and the world? The pointed question may be raised: If your congregation was closed, who (other than current members) would miss it? Congregations look strategically and practically at how they can build what Tomlinson calls "social capital" and service in their local community. Companion missioners and mentors are assigned to journey with congregations, helping them to focus on education and mission.

In Scotland, local collaborative ministry has taken root mostly in remote areas: the Highlands and Islands and the rural areas of Galloway

---

MINISTRY DEVELOPMENT IN CONGREGATIONS

COMPETENCY FRAMEWORK FOR CONGREGATIONAL USE
Areas of congregational life being developed:

1. We are becoming critical and creative theological reflectors.
2. We are learning how to resource ourselves and others theologically.
3. We are working on developing our understanding of ministry of servanthood.
4. We are working on our skills as sensitive communicators.
5. We are resourcing ourselves to grow as contemplative disciples.
6. We are learning to work collaboratively.
7. We are learning to deal critically with structures, power, and authority.
8. We are learning how to monitor our needs as a congregation.

This is the task of the Church. This is our task: to live and work for the Kingdom of God.

Scottish Episcopal Church. Used with permission.

---

and the Scottish Borders. A few small urban churches have taken on an LCM ethos, and a small church in Dundee has become engaged in this process. In all, twenty-one congregations are fully on board with LCM, while another twenty or so are working in various stages with assigned mentors, educating themselves about various aspects of shared ministry. Several members of LCM congregations have been commissioned for various responsibilities. Unlike Northern Michigan, however, only a few people have been identified for ordained local ministry. Many communities have a resident priest in their midst, are supported by retired clergy, or both, and others are moving toward becoming self-sustaining bodies. The education of those that have been identified for ordination occurs locally as much as possible with competencies met through an Individual Development Plan.

One vibrant example of local common ministry is St. John's Church, Rothiemurchus. Located amid the stunning scenery of the Cairngorms National Park in the Scottish Highlands, this picturesque white-framed church is settled in a quiet forest glade. The members of St. John's have been working on living into their responsibilities as baptized Christians.

About forty in number, they have since 1996 undertaken continued study, developed a mission in the local community that involves recycling furniture for those in need, and confidently identified a person in their midst to be trained as a locally ordained minister. Five other members of the congregation studied alongside her as they too became more knowledgeable about their own identified ministries. One member focused on hospitality, another on administration. Together they speak not primarily of increased numerical growth, but rather on "increased closeness to God, and increased responsibility for all members for His work."[21]

The primary focus in Scotland, as we have seen, is developing the congregation's life both in and out of the church building. Each congregation's overall participation in God's mission is assessed through annual reviews of its health, spirituality, mission, and ministry. These investigations are characterized by the concern with quality not quantity, by the presence of an external facilitator to ensure objectivity and affirmation, by an open process that involves the whole congregation, by telling stories of new insights, and by affirming the positive. Those present at the review openly reflect on eight competencies for the whole congregation (see the sidebar "Ministry Development in Congregations" on page 117). For example, three areas for assessment are: "We are learning how to resource ourselves and others theologically," "We are learning to work collaboratively," and "We are learning to deal critically with structures, power, and authority." This valuable and specific framework for congregational development affirms people's pride in their congregation and addresses in concrete ways their daily living within and beyond the church. Confidence and dignity among individual participants, as well as a renewed sense of each setting's distinctive mission, shape LCM congregations.

In 2008 a group of independent consultants conducted a major review of local collaborative ministry's practices and policies in the Scottish Episcopal Church. This review recommended that LCM educational practices and mission-centered church development be mainstreamed throughout the church, rather than assumed to be effective only for small congregations.[22] The stories of the journeys travelled by twenty-one LCM parishes have been compiled in an attractive pamphlet, *Local Collaborative Ministry: The Story So Far.*[23] Here congregational members bear witness to the value of educational resources, new mission endeavors, the immense energy and enthusiasm of participants, future commitments, and signs of the Spirit at work in their midst. LCM congregations are evangelistic, looking to encourage others who might be interested in stepping into this new experience of faithful living.

LCM congregations have also hosted their own visitors' weekends. This opportunity for mutual learning was similar to Northern Michigan's practice, except perhaps for oatcakes and Scottish dancing. Participants came from a Norwegian Lutheran congregation, from Wales, and from mission-focused organizations in England. One visitor observed appreciatively that LCM congregations even in the "tiniest breakthroughs" have "built up a wealth of wise experience about what encourages the growth of healthy, flourishing Christian community."[24] These visitors spoke about hearing powerful stories of a "church emerging in the midst of old structures and practices."[25] Scotland's local collaborative ministry congregations are leading others to experience what Anne Tomlinson describes as a "communication reversal." She observes people are learning "to hear and heed the voices of small and often geographically marginal congregations. They have become the prophets, speaking out of their vulnerability and so-called weakness, challenging the more prosperous and comfortable congregations, and modeling a new way of being church."[26]

Skilled educators are shaping Scotland's experience of congregational development. LCM congregations, grounded in education offered to all, are enthusiastically modeling principles of shared ministry and increasing collaboration, while offering their wisdom to larger congregations and denominations.

MOVING SHARED MINISTRY
FROM MAINTENANCE TO MISSION

Many congregations in the Episcopal Diocese of Wyoming have a different story to tell. Their journey in ministry development may have started with a paucity of financial resources and full-time clergy who were getting bored, rusting out (not burning out), and leaving small congregations after a short tenure. Churches were calling clergy who didn't stay very long. Churches were not growing or having a visible presence within the wider community. In some cases, professionally educated clergy assigned to small settings were overwhelming laity and unintentionally building up passive structures. A "father knows best" assumption was at work in some settings. Typically with 90 percent of a congregation's budget assigned to clergy salary and benefits, and 10 percent to keep the lights on, no room was left to support either education or mission. When Bruce Caldwell, the new bishop, arrived in 1997 he found in most places a model of ministry that was neither healthy nor sustainable for Wyoming's small, often isolated congregations. Dealing with smaller congregations was stated as a priority in his position description. Some people were open to new insights and experiences. Meanwhile, he found that although there were congregations in more populated areas following the traditional model with full-time clergy, many more congregations with ten to seventy members were in flux. A number were in smaller communities and designated as "missions" and largely dependent upon funding from the judicatory. The expectation and standard for survival in many of these self-consciously marginal churches were at best described as "just getting by." Many were also experiencing a spiritual drought. "Clergy come and go," one longtime resident reported. "We stay and 'pick up the pieces.'"

Today, more than a decade later, forty-eight Episcopal congregations are widely scattered across Wyoming's vast terrain. Like Northern Michigan, distances between congregations are considerable, making clustering impractical. Yet this judicatory has managed to support and revitalize congregations across the state. In fact there is an Episcopal congregation in every town (but one) with a population over one thousand. Unlike Northern Michigan, Wyoming relies on a combination of full-time, traditionally ordained clergy and voluntary, locally ordered clergy. All congregations are committed to a standard of vitality grounded theologically in baptism. Several large congregations have full-time seminary-trained clergy. Twenty-seven of the smaller congregations now practice *shared ministry*, terminology they use alternatively with *mutual ministry*. More congregations are considering this model. It is structured so that a full-time, professionally trained ministry developer works collaboratively with congregations in each of the six regions. These congregations have committed to a partnering relationship with the judicatory. Partnering congregations contribute a 50 percent assessment to the judicatory to develop and support local mutual ministry. This payment is far less that the almost 90 percent of a typical small parish's budget that was previously devoted to clergy salary and benefits.

Within the wider ministry development movement, the Wyoming story is exemplary in several respects. First, lessons can be drawn from the theology that propelled this movement over the past twelve years as well as the wisdom found in daily practices. Judicatory leaders are also pursuing a new direction for congregational vitality, emphasizing a shift from maintenance to mission, both for partnering and for traditionally structured congregations. The major challenge ahead is for self-sustaining congregations to become self-propagating, releasing energies for mission outward into the local community and region. The strategy and theology engaged in additional stages of congregational development are worth analyzing.

Bruce Caldwell is a plainspoken, direct communicator who brings a background in community organizing to his role as bishop. Before coming to Wyoming, he contributed in imaginative ways to parish settings. In one congregation he introduced intergenerational circus games, in another the local church shared its space during the week with a ballet school. Caldwell had also worked as a missioner in Alaska and was aware of the history of mutual ministry there. Like the English missionary Roland Allen, Caldwell's theology is saturated with a sense of the Spirit's energy. In a DVD describing his theology, Caldwell points to the Spirit's abundant power working underneath the body of the church. Drawing upon the epistles of Paul, especially Ephesians, he speaks of the Spirit's power conveyed through baptism into the body of God's people. Caldwell also describes ministry development as a spiritual movement that is a continuation of the Reformation. Then as now, people take ownership of their faith in new ways and claim their gifts with authority. For Caldwell, "baptism is at the heart and soul of it all," enlivening a spiritual power already present even in the smallest community.[27] One of the central components of the Diocese of Wyoming's regional ministry development is serving as a companion and guide for the local congregation as members identify the spiritual power already in their midst.

When Caldwell arrived in Wyoming a decade ago, the seeds for ministry development had been planted in two small communities. He moved to reorganize the judicatory in systematic ways, encouraging many more congregations to consider mutual ministry. Caldwell was aware from prior experience that models of shared ministry, baptismal ministry, or mutual ministry need ongoing support to thrive and last.

He notes frequently that this "would not be an easy, simple, or quick fix." The plan for ministry development involved changed staffing patterns, procedures, and financial commitments. From the beginning, a large portion of the judicatory budget was directed to support congregations as they explored and gradually adopted this alternative model. Most entered the process of mutual ministry out of financial need and fear about surviving. "It's this way or the highway," as one newcomer to shared ministry initially observed. Later on she discovered that mutual ministry is not actually about the money, rather it is about community formation. Exploring shared ministry involved frank and realistic conversations between judicatory and congregational leaders about the sustainability of the traditional model of ministry. Conflicts were worked through as prior parish histories were reviewed. New steps toward shared ministry were typically tentative. They required careful attention and pastoral care, plus sustained educational formation. Each congregation's evolution to mutual ministry took time, a three- to five-year period in most places. Caldwell has advised others considering shared ministry in their own contexts to be prepared to commit a great deal of time, energy, and resources to this work. He insists that this is "a major change that is not to be played with."[28]

In spite of all the effort required, the rewards of this kind of ministry can be great. Communities that formerly considered themselves marginal have a new sense of vitality and pride. People talk about a "sense of fulfillment in answering God's call," whatever their own gift may be. They find "real honor" in being asked to serve in a particular role, whether as a layperson or in a locally ordained capacity. Countless individuals in Wyoming, as in Northern Michigan and Scotland, testify to their deepening faith and awareness of their responsibilities as Christians. Insights from mutual ministry congregations are that everybody is gifted with the authority given in baptism, respect for one another is fundamental, and the Spirit is at work in their midst. They are able to look to the future with a sense of abundance rather than scarcity. In spite of these valuable achievements, shared ministry is not primarily about individuals taking on new roles as volunteers on a collaborative team. The most pervasive shifts are communal. Sustainability depends on the spiritual health of the whole congregation.

It is important that shared ministry congregations do not become stuck looking inward. Judicatory leaders have observed that some congregations, who are increasingly adept at building interdependence within, are not engaging interdependently with the wider community. Shared ministry has not always led inevitably to outward growth and gospel proclamation. In short, some congregations have spent more time maintaining community than growing community. Of course this limitation is not restricted to congregations that embrace ministry development. It can become a significant stumbling block for all. Margaret Babcock, a diocesan staff person with responsibility for ministry development, uses the analogy of an "unbalanced washing machine that wobbles and clunks along."[29] Too much effort is spent on one "side," focusing on worship and building pastoral care within. The load needs to be intentionally rebalanced. Other baptismal promises, promises about resisting evil, proclaiming the gospel, serving others, and striving for widespread justice, mercy, and respect for all, need more than rhetorical observance. Babcock employs community-organizing skills within church structures. She is attuned to fostering health in the congregation as well as the wider community. Her image for the role of a ministry developer is that of an environmentalist.[30] The primary job is creating a healthy milieu from which the leadership of others can blossom. This involves helping the community understand their ground or context, removing weeds or obstacles in the way, deeply rooting opportunities for growth, and nurturing healthy relationships.

Congregations in Wyoming, both partnering and traditional, are encouraged to readdress their attention and to focus on growing community. The intentional goal is to release imagination for mission so that congregations will become self-propagating within their local communities. Judicatory leaders are offering regional opportunities for equipping leaders with skills and tools for community development, mission and outreach, and evangelism. In addition, thanks to a generous bequest, a local foundation in 2008 gave each congregation a "mustard seed" grant of twelve thousand dollars to stimulate mission.[31] This judicatory believes that investing in its people will further local mission and trusts those in local congregations to discern and make decisions about the shape of those ministries.

The congregation of All Saints Church, Wheatland, Wyoming, located about an hour from Cheyenne, embodies the movement from shared ministry toward wider mission. A decade ago this small member church was in danger of losing its presence in the community. Early in that decade it embraced mutual ministry. Today it has progressed from a being a dysfunctional family with a dictator father into a community with choices, multiple leaders, new energy, and deeper commitment among parishioners. Enthusiasm in this congregation is now evident among all of its generations. In addition, All Saints Church is well connected in the wider community. Joel Dingman, its first locally ordained priest, had day jobs as the mayor of Wheatland and a full-time supervisor at the nearby power plant.[32] Members of this congregation speak of accepting their authority, ownership, and responsibility for parish leadership. More recently, they have been pursuing a community-organizing model. They hired a community organizer and studied unmet needs for service and justice in wider Wheatland. After deciding to work on decreasing bullying in the local schools, they worked with youth leaders at the diocese's summer camp to strengthen their sense of community and teamwork. In a short time members have learned that bullying is down and student grades are up. Their work with young people in the wider community also includes partnering junior high students as mentors with adults on how to use cell phones, computers, and other technological challenges. Caldwell describes the movement within All Saints Church as "stimulating an imagination for mission." Theologically he repeatedly refers to baptismal promises to proclaim new life in Christ in word and deed. "Bringing new things to life is a Resurrection promise."[33]

The story of moving from maintenance to mission is not a new one. A distinct innovation in the Diocese of Wyoming is the formation of regional "apostolic teams." Apostolic leadership is traditionally associated with bishops and other judicatory heads. Wyoming's bishop sees his role as one of oversight across a large area. He has described an apostolic leader as having "the eye of the eagle." Caldwell insists that every community has people who are gifted as apostles. These people have the ability to see the big picture, listen, communicate, and collaborate with others in open-minded ways. Leaders from each congregation in a region will comprise a regional apostolic team. By utilizing this structure, Wyoming is inviting a type of shared episcopacy. Not surprising is that, given their experience of mutual ministry at the congregational level, judicatory leaders in both Wyoming and Northern Michigan are now moving to situate aspects of episcopacy in shared group leadership.

A similar regional strategy for advancing evangelism and mission, with a focus wider than an individual congregation, has begun in the Episcopal Diocese of Northern California. Their strategy of "area ministry" has been introduced to connect churches, institutions, and people to identify fresh expressions of mission.[34] Embracing the wider community, area, or region is an increasingly significant aspect of ministry development.

ALTERNATIVE EDUCATIONAL FORMATION

As we have seen throughout regions engaged in ministry development, providing broadly accessible educational resources is a pivotal component of ministry development. For ministry development to be successful short and long term, attention needs to be paid to the education and spiritual formation of each local congregation. Because ministry development shifts the emphasis from an individual's ministry to that of the community, educational resources are typically designed for group learning. Whenever possible, preparation for various ministries—lay and ordained—takes place and is evaluated within a group setting. A basic principle is the commitment to offering education for all. Once again, principles from the English missionary Roland Allen are put to use. Allen underscored the dignity and responsibility of the learning community. He insisted on letting a local community make its own decisions, even against the advice of their teacher: "It would be far better that our converts fall into mistakes . . . than that their sense of responsibility be undermined."[35] Following the apostle Paul, Allen maintained that the test of good teaching was in its practical and positive use for building up the community. Given the pragmatic character of community formation, it is to be expected that each course of study is adapted to the local context in its presentation, content, and duration.

This is true, for example, in the educational process entitled, *Rooted in God: Moving from Maintenance to Mission*.[36] This introduction to identifying a congregation's unique mission was designed by Wyoming's Margaret Babcock; a number of ministry developers across the United States

and Canada now use this resource. *LifeCycles*, an extensive library of resources for congregations and judicatories, has been designed specifically
for those working in ministry development.[37] Drawing upon the experience and scholarship of a collaborative team of ministry developers from
several dioceses and communities, this ongoing and flexible formation
process is intended to train people for congregational leadership. *Life-
Cycles* is broadly used as a central resource by ministry developers from
Maryland to California. The creativity and imagination of congregations
who are pursuing mutual ministry emerges as well in their homegrown
educational programs. A case in point is the multisession *Waterwings* program designed by New Song congregation in Coralville, Iowa, to introduce people to the theology and practice of baptismal ministry. Designed
for newcomers, those seeking baptism or confirmation, or those simply
wishing to learn more about mutual ministry, *Waterwings* offers an opportunity to be "buoyed [up] by the gifts that God has given us."[38] The
three programs cited above are by no means all the available courses designed for education and spiritual formation within local congregations.
From Washington State to Vermont, congregational and judicatory leaders have been using programs that respect the dignity and questions of
the adult learner. The formation process for mutual ministry teams and
congregations underscores the value of ongoing access to educational resources in the wider community. Formation is lifelong for all.

One of the major concerns that newcomers to ministry development
often have is about the preparation of those trained locally for ordained
ministries. People at all judicatory levels need to be reassured that the
education and formation of local leaders will be adequate to their responsibilities. While questions related to commissioning lay leaders are
typical, much of the unease found at the judicatory level centers primarily upon pastoral leadership. What alternative models are in use? There
is wide variety within judicatories. A few have their own local seminary
or school. Examples include an e-seminary in Iowa, summer programs in
Washington, and a variety of plans shaped around *LifeCycles* in Maryland
as well as Northern Michigan and Vermont. What these efforts have in
common is that preparation for those volunteers who are identified for
local ordination is lengthy, intentionally grounded in community, and
demanding. Most preparation takes three to five years to meet overall
judicatory requirements. While formation primarily takes place within
the local congregation, those pursuing ordained and other ministries also

participate in workshops sponsored by the judicatories, and in seminary-based courses for locally trained ministers that are delivered either on-line or in one- or two-week intensive courses.[39] Descriptions of the com-petencies for each of the several ministry roles (for example, presbyter, deacon, preacher, stewardship coordinator, ecumenical coordinator) that a congregation might identify as its ministry support team are typically available from the judicatory and online.[40] Both local and judicatory offi-cials guide the formation process. Often it is based around completion of competency-based portfolios, or learner-centered guidelines, which give each participant opportunity and flexibility in choosing and designing learning experiences. Before either local ordination or commissioning (in the case of nonordained leaders) takes place, approval and certifica-tion must be given by the judicatory. Wherever possible, these congrega-tional leaders are formed, trained, and commissioned as a group, often in a worship service replete with baptismal theology.

As the need for people who can support and companion congrega-tions engaging in ministry development has steadily grown, resources for educating regional ministry developers have increased. Most of the people working as full-time ministry developers are seminary graduates, and all but a handful are ordained. Recognizing that traditional seminary train-ing assumes a "paid clergy at the top" model, a few theological schools have collaborated with judicatory leaders to offer courses that introduce the theology and practice of ministry development. Opportunities to be immersed in the assumptions and contexts for this specialized ministry are now offered both online and on campus.[41] To guide the educational process, members of the Ministry Developers' Collaborative in 2004 is-sued a competency-based curriculum for seminarians or for postseminary continuing education. They agreed upon four central competencies for professional ministry developers that still pertain today: working with groups, working in church systems, leading and teaching theological re-flection and interpretation, and making companions in ministry.

While several of the competencies for ministry developers overlap with traditional models for clerical leadership, assumptions about pow-er, leadership, and context vary considerably. Internships and, where possible, field education sites have been helpful for those making the transition to ministry development. In 2007 a group of ministry de-velopers and seminary educators were authorized by the Living Stones Partnership to design a formal Certificate in Ministry Development. It

COMPETENCIES FOR MINISTRY DEVELOPERS

1. *Working with groups:*
   a. Uses skills of group dynamics for effective group action.
   b. Applies skills for assessment and decision making that maximize partici-pation and ownership.
   c. Applies skills for giving and eliciting feedback.
   d. Uses networking, advocacy, and political skills in wider church systems.
2. *Working in church systems:*
   a. Demonstrates congregational development skills.
   b. Conducts group consultations in congregations.
   c. Can recognize and confront unhelpful uses of power.
   d. Involves and helps others through organizational change.
3. *Leading and teaching theological reflection and interpretation:*
   a. Demonstrates skills in theological articulation and reflection.
   b. Guides theological reflection.
   c. Applies knowledge and skills of cultural differences.
   d. Engages others in Scripture study.
   e. Develops interpretive skills in others for examining social context.
   f. Leads efforts at education in ministry.
4. *Making companions in ministry:*
   a. Encourages others in using their gifts.
   b. Practices and describes ministry, office, and role so as to invite others in.
   c. Uses skills for supporting others one-on-one in ministry.
   d. Draws on personal experience and the church's tradition and resources to offer spiritual guidance.
   e. Applies self-management and self-assessment skills in a ministry devel-opment context.
5. Ongoing Cycle: *Identify, Educate, Support*

Copyright © 2004 Ministry Developers' Collaborative. Used with permission.

too will be competency based.[42] These and other efforts are designed to strengthen the education of excellent ministry developers for the future church.

Alternate paths to ordination at the local level and the profession of ministry developer itself have raised questions, challenges, and in some instances outright resistance. Some see these alternatives as threats to the status of the ordained, while some small and struggling congrega-tions still want "a man-in-charge" model. Letting go of tradition is hard, particularly in the church. Proponents of ministry development encounter questions from clergy who fear for their jobs. As presiding bishop of the Episcopal Church Katharine Jefferts Schori has affirmed, there will always be congregations that want and need full-time clergy in residence. There will also be congregations with demographically limited growth prospects who are unable to finance full-time clergy, and others for whom mutual ministry teams are ideal.[43] In the vast majority of judicatories, traditional and emerging expressions of ministry exist side by side. As leaders in the United Kingdom, New Zealand, across the United States, and elsewhere are finding, a variety of models are and will continue to be needed to serve the emerging church.

Whatever model of leadership is engaged, it is clear that accountability to baptismal ministry and increased appreciation for the gifts within gathered communities are not only biblical but also pragmatic directions for congregations of any size. A few judicatories are first exploring baptismal ministry principles and practices in their larger congregations. Their hope is not only to enhance the vitality of these congregations but also to illustrate that ministry development is not a second-class status for congregations. The gifts of the Holy Spirit are present in every congregation. One longtime practitioner of baptismal ministry, Kevin Thew Forrester, describes ministry development as "an art of recognizing the beauty and uniqueness of each baptized person and each local community."[44] Enthusiasm, commitment, responsibility, and a renewed sense of mission were visible in each of the ministry development congregations we were able to visit. The best practices that support the ministry of the baptized need to be more widely known and drawn upon for the sake of the church's overall vitality.

DISCUSSION QUESTIONS

1. Where do you see ministry developing in your congregation? How do you and others help cultivate ministry in your community of faith?

2. The importance of place is foundational for ministry development. What images or stories come to mind as you describe the place where your ministry is located? What particular strengths and future possibilities are imbedded in this place?

3. In most situations where local ministry development is successful, the congregation becomes an ongoing community of learners. What does "formation for all" mean to you?

4. A key component in successful ministry development is a congregation's partnership with the local judicatory, synod, district, presbytery, region, or diocese. What might (or does) this look like in your context?

5. In our culture and in many traditional church structures, leadership is not shared. What biblical passages directly point to the importance of shared ministerial leadership?

Chapter 4

Emergent Perspectives on the Church and Ministry

Baptismal ministry challenges us to reimagine the church and its calling. The predominate model of church organization, the church-as-institution model, has evolved over time and has served some Christian communities well. While traditionally structured congregations are critiqued as "consumer" churches where members show up on Sunday, passively participate, and then leave all the ministry for clergy to do, there are many such congregations where participation is vibrant and ministry is shared. The problem is that this model has severe limitations for congregations in locations that cannot support such churches financially or maintain full-time seminary-trained clergy. The question then becomes: are congregations without paid clergy less than full members of the body of Christ? Are local communities where demographic growth is unlikely undeserving of churches? Should the sacraments be available only where a congregation can pay someone to deliver them? Perhaps the answers to these questions lie in our ability to recognize a diversity of models of church and ministry, and our task is to apply some of the flexibility and freedom of our history in support of congregations today.

Baptismal Ecclesiology

The term *ecclesiology* comes from the Greek word *ekklesia*, commonly translated as "assembly." *Ecclesiology* means our theological understanding of the church or our way of living in community, which we already know has been interpreted from a variety of perspectives throughout Christian history. From the perspective of ministry development, ecclesiology is not simply an academic discussion. It is an important topic in that it challenges us to name clearly who we are and what we are called to do in the world. A clearly articulated understanding of ecclesiology is the foundation for our understanding of ministry and leadership.

An ecclesiology rooted in baptism binds each Christian to Christ within the body, or community, of faith. Our baptism draws us into a profound ecclesial relationship. Through our baptism we are in communion with Christ, by the power of the Spirit; we are also bound together in relationship with all other believers; and we become inseparable from the church and its mission in the world. Baptismal ecclesiology begins with the gathering of all believers. In this vision of the church, all God's people are participants in the life of the church and not passive observers. Ministries are established according to a diversity of gifts, based on a respectful mutuality, and focused outward toward the church's mission to the world. In this way, all ministers, laity and ordained, are oriented toward the reign of God. Baptismal ecclesiology believes that through each of its members, and local faith communities on the whole, the church works to heal and strengthen the whole human family. As theologian Richard Gaillardetz writes about the gathering of the baptized in local communities, "We enact, if only for an hour, a world transformed by God's shalom."[1]

Throughout the last century contemporary models of baptismal ecclesiology have emerged as parallel developments in North America, Australia, New Zealand, Southern Africa, the United Kingdom, and other parts of the world.[2] One of the first distinct modern sources was Roland Allen, who believed that the most effective way to encourage conversions was to raise up and support local indigenous leaders. At the heart of this message was Allen's belief that the mission of the church is the work of the Spirit, and that traditional mission strategies essentially frustrate and immobilize spiritual movements. Further, Allen argued that the professionalization of missions meant that the focus of the work shifted from the spread of the gospel to supporting institutions and missionaries. He wrote:

Missionary societies began their crusade, not by striving to call out the spirit of Christian men whose occupation carried them abroad, not by trying to impress on the Church at home that Christ calls *all* His people to witness for Him wherever they may be, wherever they may go, but by creating an army of professional missionaries. The whole system of societies, boards, offices, accounts, contracts with missionaries, statistical returns, reports, reeks of it. From every missionary society there goes out every day into every part of the world with one insistent unceasing voice the proclamation that the gospel must be preached by special agents maintained by a society for this particular work. No verbal denials can shake it.[3]

While Roland Allen's notion of missionary expansion is commonly accepted now, his work had little influence during his lifetime. Allen left us two books that eventually informed the evolution of baptismal ecclesiology later in the century: *Missionary Methods: St. Paul's or Ours?* (1912) and *The Spontaneous Expansion of the Church and Causes that Hinder It* (1927).

In 1960 Boone Porter, a professor at the General Theological Seminary in New York, referred Roland Allen's books to Bill Gordon, then the Episcopal bishop of Alaska, a vast region of primarily small, poor, and remote congregations. Gordon saw potential in Allen's concept of spontaneous expansion, or the belief that faith expands rapidly when people in a particular location feel free to respond out of their own initiative, in ways that reflect their own experience.[4] Gordon began an experiment by ordaining members of local communities in Alaska to preside at the Eucharist. Porter further expanded on this work by founding the Leadership Academy for New Directions in 1974, and with Wesley Frensdorff, then the Episcopal bishop of Nevada, organized the Pacific Rim Conference in 1983. The conference gathered one hundred fifty Anglicans from around the world to reflect on mission and ministry. Frensdorff became a major force in what was then commonly called the "Total Ministry" movement and was the inspiration behind its evolutionary ecclesiology. He explains the main ingredients of this ecclesiology in four points:

Firstly, that each congregation will truly be, in a self-conscious way, a ministering community rather than the community gathered around a minister. And that it will become therefore sufficient in ministry from within its own membership, that it will also raise up from within itself persons for the office of deacon and priest, as being essential for the total life and mission of the church; and. . .

Secondly, that each member therefore, of the church, will have the opportunity to serve our Lord in the church and in the world through significant ministries which will vary greatly with each member. . . . .

The third goal is that seminary-trained clergy and qualified laity will increasingly be used as trainers, and enablers, supervisors and pastors of trainees. . . .

The fourth assumption of the goal is that the diocese, as the primary unit of interdependence in the life of the church, is the support system by which congregations are interlinked and support each other.[5]

The connection between total ministry and baptismal ecclesiology was reinforced by Frensdorff's successor in Nevada, Stewart Zabriskie. Zabriskie inspired the movement and made its principles accessible to a broader audience through his popular 1995 book, *Total Ministry*. Zabriskie believed that the entire local Christian community is called to respond to the call of baptism through ministering in Christ's name. "To 'have a vocation' is to be baptized," wrote Zabriskie. "To 'go into ministry' is to be baptized. Throughout much of its history, the church has denied that vocational scope and given higher credence and respect to clergy vocations," he writes. Zabriskie believed it was essential for the church to *listen* to those who are ministering as Christ's body and to broaden its sense of vocation to ministry to include all the baptized.[6]

Liturgical scholar Louis Weil, in his writing on the theology of worship, stresses baptism as the defining sacrament of incorporation into the church's life and sees baptismal ecclesiology as what all members of the church share. Weil argues that we Christians are so used to looking at the denominational divisions that separate us, we miss the "essential unity of Christians that baptism creates."[7] He believes that much of what divides members of Christian denominations is based on matters of church organization. Baptismal ecclesiology acknowledges the diversity found within the scope of Christian history in matters of polity and governance, while at the same time upholds the unity of all Christians through baptism. "This baptismal ecclesiology thus offers a basis not only for ecumenical dialogue but also for common worship as Christians of different traditions work for the recovery of the visible unity to which the one baptism compels us."[8]

Weil's vision of baptismal ecclesiology is deeply incarnational, in that it assumes all Christians, through our baptism, are radically united in the body of Christ despite all forms of human injustice and indifference. The physical world, as the place where we encounter God and what is holy, is sacramental, and we are called to take that seriously. Weil refers to the sacramentality of the physical world found in baptismal ecclesiology as a guiding principle for each Christian in his or her ministry: "The work of the church is not to escape the world, but to be the agent of transformation and healing whenever we encounter injustice, abuse, hatred or indifference."[9]

Andy Crouch, former editor of the Christian Vision Project and former editor in chief of re:generation Quarterly, writes that "the church that baptizes together stays together—if indeed its leaders teach and live in such a way." Crouch believes that baptism is the church's most powerful response to individualism, and that the only truly postindividualistic community in our society today is the fellowship of the baptized. "To the extent that we continue to grasp for an individualistic identity, it is a sign of our failure to understand and live into our baptism." Crouch maintains that baptism is the first practice to take the Christian community beyond modernity and postmodernity, "with their equally inhuman agendas of assimilation and fragmentation. . . If baptism offers the only way into true postindividualism, the Eucharist offers the only way into true postconsumerism. If baptism addresses our distorted sense of self-hood, communion offers us a truer way to consume. For in communion we quite literally consume the most basic of goods, food and drink, and that consumption is taken up into Christ."[10]

In addition to its development in North America, baptismal ecclesiology has emerged throughout the world over the last forty years. In Australia in the 1990s, after a modest start in North Queensland, the Goldfields, and Northern Regions of Perth in Western Australia, which were home to many small and remote congregations, initiated baptismal ecclesiology under the leadership of Brian Farran. "Despite a long history of stipendiary ministry in rural and remote areas, adequate formation of the whole Church has not occurred," he writes. "The authorized leader of a local community mirrors the community itself. Thus a priest grows into being a eucharistic person, a person of thanksgiving, deeply sensitive to the holiness of all life, and perceptive of the ordinariness of God in the local context."[11]

Although congregations in the United Kingdom do not have the challenge of great distances faced by congregations in Australia, the shortage of stipendiary clergy precipitated the need for changes in the ministry delivery system of the church. Through local ministry development, more than one thousand local clergy were ordained roughly between 1970 and 1990. At the same time, a new paradigm of shared ministry began to evolve in local congregations. Robin Greenwood, former director of ministry for the Church in Wales, and now the vicar of Monkseaton in the Diocese of Newcastle, writes about a "new ecclesiology of inclusiveness." This model of ecclesiology focuses on developing local ministry teams of stipendiary and nonstipendiary clergy and laity. One source estimates that more than half of the parishes in the United Kingdom are in some way associated with team ministry.[12]

The experience of basic ecclesial communities in Latin America, also known as base Christian communities, continues to inform the baptismal ecclesiology movement. Within Latin America, basic ecclesial communities have paved the way for transforming the pastoral vision of the church. By definition, such communities are first *basic*, growing from the faith of ordinary baptized people; second, *ecclesial*, continuing the prophetic mission of Jesus and the Holy Spirit; and last, *community*, in communion with God, with others, and with history. Such communities are seen as a manifestation of the Holy Spirit and a means to purify the entire church so that it can more authentically speak to the realities of people at the grassroots, transform everyday realities, alleviate practices that no longer support mission, and realign resources to focus on the church's mission as a sacramental event within a process of global renewal. Overall, the basic ecclesial community sees itself as an extension of the reign of God into the world. As Jose Marins writes, "The basic ecclesial community is not an end in itself; otherwise it would cease to be leaven; it would cease to be Church and would become merely a sect. The goal of the basic ecclesial community is the extension of the Kingdom of God. It is not a place of quiet, isolated refuge, but rather for deepening and intensifying faith and commitment."[13]

Theologians and pastors associated with the base ecclesial community movement suggest that important characteristics distinguish a *community* from a *group* or another form of social structure such as an organization. A basic ecclesial community is an intentional *theological* community, not simply a sociological or psychological one. The language of base ecclesial communities suggests that many North American churches more closely operate as groups, rather than as theological communities. For instance, in the base ecclesial community context, a community is an expression of permanence and stability, whereas a group is transitory and ceases to exist when its reason for existence is no longer evident. Within the base ecclesial community, the focus of concern encompasses all of human life—religion, family, education, health, social issues, politics, leisure—whereas a group is specialized and responds to a particular aspect of human life, such as religion. A community within the basic ecclesial community model is pluralistic, bringing together a diversity of people in age, gender, culture, social class, religious practice, called to work together toward common goals in service of the whole. On the other hand, groups tend to be homogeneous, consisting of people of the same age, cultural background, and language, and tend toward uniformity. Moreover, within the basic ecclesial community model, the goal is to build friendships through an intimacy and openness toward all, avoiding the formation of exclusive groups and intimacy restricted to certain members.[14]

COMMUNITY	GROUP
Global	Specialized
Permanent	Transitory
Pluralistic	Uniform
Friendship/Relationships	Exclusive

Adapted from Jose Marins, Carolee Chanona, Teolide Trevisan, The Church from the Roots: Basic Ecclesial Communities (Quezon City: Phil.: Claretian, 1997), 30–31.

The similarities between the ecclesiologies of base Christian communities and the baptismal ministry movement are evident. Both the basic ecclesial community and the baptismal ecclesiology movements reinforce the belief that people in local communities are most empowered when they genuinely share in a collaborative vision of ministry rooted in the local context, yet are linked with a broader vision and sense of common mission. Both models stress genuine community as a deep and vital relationship between members based in solidarity and mutual help. Similarly, both models stress the sanctity of daily life and the importance of facing challenges and transforming them through Christian hope. Further, both movements use training methods that value the experience and stories of the local community and use and support the gifts of the community. They de-emphasize formal structures over establishing a way of communal living that invites participation and broader leadership. Finally, they seek radical change by balancing the church-as-institution model with the workings of the Spirit in a particular local congregation at a particular time.[15]

The Church as the People of God

The late Verna J. Dozier, an educator and advocate for the ministry of the baptized, wrote about the differences between perceptions of the church as an institution and the church as the people of God. Dozier was a lifelong churchgoer and leader in congregations, and she believed profoundly that even when the church acts out of creative tension with its institutional status and gets into "the liberation business," it still falls short of its calling. "But there is more than that creative tension," she writes. "That is the best a Church as institution can do. The Church as the People of God can do more. It can change the world. But that Church is a sleeping giant, and that Church must be unbound."[16]

Dozier's ecclesiology was formed by her deep knowledge and love of Scripture, her belief that Jesus called the whole people of God to witness to the ends of the earth, and her conviction that what the church needs most is to shift its organizational structures away from institutional hierarchy. "What happens on Sunday morning is not half so important as what happens on Monday morning," she writes. "In fact what happens on Sunday morning is judged by what happens on Monday morning. If the people who gather for word and sacrament go back to the world unchanged and unchanging, they have participated in empty ritual."[17]

Dozier believed that those who are called to enact Christ's reconciling mission in the world, offering themselves in sacrificial mission, are the "priesthood of the laity." In this vision, Dozier believed that the role of the ordained is to equip the saints, to support the laity in their call to mission in the world, and to "enable laypeople to know who they are, tend the holy fire before which their souls may be rekindled when the flame burns low." Dozier writes, "There are no second-class citizens in the household of God. . . . Religious authority comes with baptism, and it is nurtured by prayer, worship, Bible study, life together." In fact, Dozier writes, it is when the people are acting in the world through wisdom and love that "the priest knows his/her ministry in the Church, the institution, has been to the glory of God."[18]

Ecclesiology should always respond to the local context and culture and be mission- and world-centered, rather than focused on preserving and maintaining particular institutional structures. The congregations and judicatories of vast regions with limited resources do not have the luxury of surplus seminary-trained clergy, extensive committee structures, or corporate programs needed to support the church-as-institution model, nor could such a model of church and ministry be sustained in such regions in the foreseeable future. Rather, sustainability for small local congregations in these regions depends on models of the church and ministry that support the formation and education of all the baptized as the ministers of God's saving love in their families and communities. A common need in these small congregations interested in recovering the ministry of the baptized is to broaden perspectives on the church and ministry. Where a congregation views the church primarily as an institution, formation and education is needed to make the paradigm shift to viewing the church as the people of God. From the perspective of baptismal ministry, the authority for ministry comes with baptism. Early Christian communities of the baptized were creative in accommodating movement and change. We cannot do less today if we wish not only to survive but also to thrive in challenging settings. If the church, as the people of God, is to thrive and grow, our structures of governance need reshaping to accommodate changing perspectives of the church and ministry.

EMBRACING THE TRINITY IN NORTHERN MICHIGAN

The Episcopal Diocese of Northern Michigan is a judicatory that has been deliberately engaged in changing models of the church and ministry since the mid-1980s. At that time, the diocese simply could no longer financially sustain conventional judicatory or congregational models. In

---

DIFFERING PERSPECTIVES ON THE CHURCH AND MINISTRY

ASSUMPTIONS ABOUT THE CHURCH VIEWED ONLY AS INSTITUTION

- Church refers to a building or an organization.
- Clergy are usually set apart from laity.
- The church is institutionally self-centered.
- Members have a deep-rooted pessimism about humanity.
- People worry about working out their salvation.
- The laity are objects of religious care and consumers of sacramental products.
- The ethos is that of an individualistic Greek world, which must be preserved and kept in order.
- Officials legitimate and parcel out activities.
- The church consists of priest-centered ministries delivered to troubled laity.
- Emphasis is on learned clergy and "professional" ministry.

ASSUMPTIONS ABOUT THE CHURCH VIEWED PRIMARILY AS PEOPLE OF GOD

- *Church* means Christians, the people of God.
- Christians are clergy and laity assembled for the purposes of worship and mission.
- The church is mission centered and world centered.
- Members believe that God's grace perfects nature.
- God has already acted for us in Christ Jesus.
- Christians are *agents*, the signs and bearers of God's saving love.
- The ethos is that of a corporate *Hebraic* world, accustomed to movement and change.
- Members experience spontaneous expansion and corporate witness.
- The church consists of Christ-centered people at work in a troubled world.
- Emphasis is on educated Christians and baptismal ministry.

Adapted from Fredrica Harris Thompsett, *Ministry Development Journal*, no. 8, 1985; revised January 2005.

---

addition, theological changes with the 1979 *Book of Common Prayer* in the Episcopal Church and the ecumenical liturgical movement of the 1960s and 1970s, with the renewed emphasis on the ministry of the baptized and the centrality of the Eucharist as the primary expression of the gathered community, evoked a theology that nurtured and sustained a transforming movement within the diocese. At the same time, diocesan leaders became aware of the negative effects of consumer-oriented culture on the church's understanding of community. "We had become people gathered around a minister, with the expectation of paying to receive a divine service," says Kevin Thew Forrester, a ministry developer in the diocese. "We were convinced that the countercultural movement of Jesus invited us into becoming adults gathered into ministering communities." The primary question became, says Thew Forrester, "How do we set a table in the wilderness, for that is precisely what we are being invited to do. It was clear, however, that not any kind of table would do. The question was how do 'we' set the table, and not, how does someone else set the table for us." Thus, new models of the church and ministry go beyond the need to help small, rural, isolated congregations survive; they also offer ways to identify, call forth, and form indigenous leadership. "Economics should not dictate sound theology and ways of life," says Thew Forrester. "Rather, sound theology and ecclesiology invite us to rework our economic structure so that it can support the gifts for ministry with which the Spirit has endowed us."[19]

One of the images used in the Diocese of Northern Michigan to envision the church and ministry is the Trinity. "The relational and nesting character of all creation reveals a communitarian approach to God, reflective of the Trinity. A creation of interwoven lives leads us to affirm that relationship, partnership, and mutuality lie at the heart of being creatures of God. When we follow this communitarian path to God, it transforms our relationship with creation," states a 2009 document the diocese published, called "A Theological Framework for the Mission Strategy of the Diocese of Northern Michigan," and edited by Thew Forrester. Although Christians in the West are accustomed to individualism, many other cultures, as well as scientists and social theorists, support the notion that no creature is ever truly singular. All creatures are interconnected and interrelated in the web of life. "The Trinity is not only how God is, it is also how we, created in God's image, rest in and come to God. God is community and so are we. A theology of mutual ministry asks us not to begin with a singular one, but with a oneness birthed through a union of mutual love."[20]

The "open and embracing love" of the Trinity is characteristic of the evolving ecclesiology of the Diocese of Northern Michigan, as well integral to the theological understanding of mutual ministry there. "Mutual ministry endeavors to embody in community life the same mutual respect eternally present in the life of God. The Trinity is a symbolic way of affirming the hope expressed in John's gospel that "*all may be one, as you, Abba, are in me and I am in you*" (17:21).[21]

Within the Diocese of Northern Michigan, baptism represents the basic response to God's invitation to new life, as well as our acceptance that we are God's own forever. "Baptism is never abstract, but always embodied in a particular life, formed in the way of Christ, inspired by the Spirit. . . . Each and every life represents a specific current within the common baptismal waters." Given this framework for baptismal living and ministry, the ordained are in no way set apart from the flow of the baptismal waters. Rather, the historic threefold order of ministry (deacon, presbyter, and bishop) is viewed as "ministerial archetypes" that reveals the order already expressed throughout baptismal living:

> The church is then the baptized and there is no such discrete and separate entity as *laity*. Each and every person is baptized into mission to the world through ministry—ministry, which is the shape of the concrete life lived in the Spirit. The traditional threefold orders [bishop, priest, deacon] reflect back to us some of the primal, or archetypal, shapes, which each and every Christian life takes. There are teachers in Christ, lawyers in Christ, janitors in Christ—but it is always some particular life in Christ that is baptized. In this way it is impossible to sever baptism from mission and ministry. Christian life is baptism into mission through ministry. To live in the baptismal waters is only possible by flowing in some distinct way—each and every life is a current or ordering of grace for mission in creation.[22]

The Diocese of Northern Michigan's vision of the church and ministry is described by the term *mutual ministry* as an expression of the community's response to trinitarian love. "Mutuality never implies sameness, rather it revels in the richness of diversity through which love is embodied and expressed. Mutuality does not simply tolerate diversity, it cultivates and celebrates the kaleidoscopic diversity as revelatory of the munificent presence of the Spirit in creation." Leadership, of first response, in mutual ministry is viewed as "midwifery of giftedness for mission." Formation for leadership begins with the awareness that God dwells in us and throughout all creation; to be human is to be of God. "Leaders live and act as midwives of the holy already present. Leaders, steeped in the wisdom of the tradition, work collaboratively with community so that gifts may re-birth God's presence. . . . Leaders, in this sense, are the midwives of a community of right relationship."[23]

The theological emphasis on the Trinity in the ecclesiology of the Diocese of Northern Michigan is a symbol of the way, through baptism, that members of faith communities are "willing to receive each other into our lives as holy presence." Through baptism the faithful accept "that we have always been and will ever be God's own, as is every creature." The diocese recognizes that the mission and ministry in a particular place is the responsibility of the people of God in that place, and seeks to *develop* those ministries, rather than *send* ministry to a community as a seminary-trained professional. Rather, seminary-trained individuals serve as resources for the ongoing formation and education of the whole people of God. In all cases, the diocese seeks to honor and support the uniqueness of the people of God and each local community:

> Leadership draws upon each one's unique set of gifts, encouraging and nurturing the trinitarian partnership amongst God's people in all areas. Leadership is always seeking to support the daily Christian responsibility of all members of the community wherever they find themselves called to share in the priestly ministry of reconciliation, the diaconal ministry of servanthood, and the apostolic ministry of oversight, reflection, and witness.[24]

Robin Greenwood, in his work on ministry teams, also holds up the image of the Trinity as the way to describe how we relate to one another and to the world through the church. Greenwood believes that within church communities the key to all relationships can be found in the image of the Trinity, including mutuality, interdependence, love, and justice. Further, he suggests that study and reflection on the Trinity, or the image of God as three persons in community, has the capacity to challenge and change how we are the church. Trinitarian life not only changes the way we relate to each other, but also changes our values and structures. As urban missioner David Clark writes, "We are called to be partners with God in his continuing work of creation within the personal, corporate and global spheres of life. We are called to be partners with Christ as he frees and empowers individuals, institutions and nations to fulfill their God-given possibilities. We are called to be partners with the spirit as she works for justice, peace and the unity of humankind. We are called to be partners with all those who work to further human dignity with the bounds of our common humanity."[25]

A STREAM RUNS FREE IN VERMONT

Thomas Clark Ely, bishop of the Episcopal Diocese of Vermont, used the image of a stream running free as a metaphor for changing perspectives on the church and ministry as he spoke to the annual convention of the diocese in 2008. Ely's address recalls a story first reported on Vermont Public Radio by John Dillon about a stream in Northfield, Vermont, about to run free for the first time in seventy years after the removal of a crumbling dam from Cox Brook, a tributary of the Dog River. Although some people in the region miss the old swimming hole created by the dam, its removal opens up miles of spawning habitat for wild trout. The Dog River is one of the few Vermont streams not stocked with fish raised in a hatchery. Wild trout need clean, running water to spawn, and thus restoring the stream opened up the possibility of new life. While the project was underway, construction workers were concerned for both the river and the fish. Trapped fish were scooped up in hard hats and laid gently downstream. Ely spoke to the way the story reminds him of the church and ministry:

> What captured my imagination was the picture of new life being made possible when the debris of a neglected dam was removed. The story points to the future and new possibilities for sustaining both habitat and life created by the removal of a crumbling dam, even though it has served a different and worthwhile purpose for some in days gone by. There was, as well, the delightful description of those construction workers and their concern *and action* on behalf of the fish.
>
> The story of the Cox Brook running free for the first time in seventy years reminds me how important it is for us to be open to the changes and chances of God's future, both for our diocese and for the planet. God hungers for us to be able to run free and give birth to new life. It reminds me of the importance of stewardship in every dimension of our lives. And it speaks to the deep concern and compassion for all creation built into the DNA of the human spirit.[26]

Since 2001, the Episcopal Diocese of Vermont has developed models of church and ministry that support the region and emphasize baptismal ministry. When Ely came to the diocese that year, he put in place a decentralized diocesan staffing model called the "Ministry Support Team," which focuses on assisting congregations. Three part-time ministry developers work out of their homes in different parts of the state. The ministry developers each have different and complementary gifts and skills, and minister in different congregations depending on the need, although they more often closely relate to congregations in their proximity. Tom Ely meets with the ministry developers every other week for a full day of team building and conversation related to their mutual ministry in the congregations of the diocese. Ely says that, although it has been hard to work through people's notion of a traditional diocesan staff rather than ministry developers focused on supporting congregations, he sees that "gradually people are growing to appreciate the concept of a support team."[27] The full team meets every six weeks.

Thaddeus Bennett, canon for ministry development and deployment of the Diocese of Vermont and part-time rector of the small rural congregation of St. Mary's, Wilmington, says, "We are definitely organizing around a diocesan-wide, regional, and local plan for ministry. The 'Episcopal See' or diocesan office in Burlington is no longer the center. We are clear that the center is where the people of God are, and we (diocesan folk) need to go where they are. Programs and systems are adapted to meet the needs there. For instance, our deployment process for 23 congregations in the last 3 years probably used 9 different models of working with lay leaders . . . the exciting work is fitting the 'basics' of deployment, which everyone really does need to pay attention to, to the size and circumstances of the congregation."

Susan Ohlidal, pastoral enrichment coordinator for the Diocese of Vermont, affirms that the new clergy-calling process is a sign of a new level of partnership between the diocese and congregations, as opposed to the older "the bishop sent us a clergyperson" model. "I cannot imagine a diocese opening up their clergy search process to this kind of review unless the governance systems and structures within the diocese are authentically and genuinely committed to all the ministries of the baptized: to hearing, valuing, and then implementing the changes brought forth by the wisdom . . . of pastoral leaders in parishes; and to take the risk that 'the way we have always done this' may no longer apply nor even be good enough any longer."

One surprising result from the new clergy-calling process in the Diocese of Vermont was a widened perspective among members of the rural congregations involved, as well as a sense of greater connection with the diocese. "We heard favorable things as well as what we need to do better and what demands continued refinement or total trashing and creating anew," says Ohlidal. "Hearing others' stories of their experience with the process led to feeling less isolated in this very rural diocese and as if 'no one' has done it before." Ohlidal believes that the review and revision of the ministry development processes of the diocese will be continuous, "reflecting the changing ministries and needs of the parishes as they, in partnership with the bishop and the diocese, discern and call new clergy leaders."[28]

Ely notes that the Diocese of Vermont already has several examples of the ministry support team model operating in congregations, and various conversations going on with other faith communities about how to move in this direction. On the congregational level, the ministry support team works in concert with the vestry, which maintains their canonical responsibilities. The ministry support teams tend to focus on responsibility for pastoral care, liturgy, and education. The concept of a team, rather than an individual, helps foster a deeper sense of community not only among members of the team but also among members of the congregation as a whole.

Ely believes that current Episcopal canons continue to restrict the roles of laity and clergy. He would like to see them open up, allowing more possibilities in judicatory and congregational structures, including ministry support teams. "I think less restrictive language on organizational models for faith communities might open up some creative thinking about structures for ministry. I think we still need some clarity and structure for congregations, but opening up (canonically) the possibility of other ways might help." Ely also sees the need for a more expansive vision that would encourage starting new congregations following a model that might not fit the status quo, yet responds to the local context's ministry and structure.[29]

Over the past eight years, the Diocese of Vermont's commitment to baptismal ministry has grown, committing itself to expanding the vitality of every congregation and to working with community, ecumenical, and interfaith partners "to bring about God's reign for a hurting world struggling for its very breath." Currently the diocese is exploring projects focusing on the environmental crisis of climate change and in global reconciliation through the United Nations Millennium Development Goals and the Anglican Communion. Throughout the Diocese of Vermont, small and often financially struggling congregations are called to live into their *abundance* and form deeper relationships within their own communities and the larger world. "Make these relationships a central part of your life as faith communities," said Tom Ely in his diocesan convention address. "This involvement is not in place of your local and domestic mission and outreach efforts, but in addition. Again, it is drawing on our abundance and generosity to break open the dams of our own hearts so that life giving water can flow freely and fully from us to spawn the new life that will come as a result."[30]

MOVING FROM COMMITTEES TO LOCAL MINISTRY TEAMS

Linda L. Grenz, founder and CEO of LeaderResources, works with many congregations and judicatories interested in changing perspectives on church and ministry. "My work with congregations has been focused around moving from *committees* to *ministries*," she says. "You need a few (but only a few) committees, e.g., finance and property. But the rest need to be ministry teams: education, communication, pastoral care, liturgy, etc." Grenz believes that ministry teams address the changing roles between clergy and laity—"a move from the priest or pastor as the primary leader who does all (or most) of the ministry (or at least the most important parts) to a shared ministry with lots of people involved in a fairly quickly changing environment which provides lots of entry points for people entering the community."[31]

CHARACTERISTICS OF EFFECTIVE MINISTRY TEAMS

- They have a clear sense of their work as ministry.
- They focus on "doing" rather than "meeting."
- The team is both responsible and accountable; i.e., it has authority to make decisions, spend money allocated to them, communicate with the congregation, develop and recommend budgets, plans, strategies, etc.
- Laity and clergy trust and support the team, rather than second-guessing; the focus is on "results" rather than who has the power to make certain decisions.
- Decisions are made in practical ways (we do this because it works right now) without expectation that the decision is perfect and will become immutable policy.
- Major decisions are made using discernment rather than politics.
- Team members move in and out of leadership roles regularly, recruit and train new members to prevent burnout, and share ministry. Leadership is shared between two people or more and cliques are avoided.
- Team members are called into ministry rather than relying on volunteers. Volunteers need to come through the same discernment process and be open to various ministries depending on what they and the discernment team sense is God's leading.
- Clergy exercise the roles of ministry developer: trainer, equipper, encourager, supporter, etc., and see ministry team members as valuable peers in the congregation.

Developed by Linda L. Grenz, founder and CEO of LeaderResources. Used with permission.

Changing perspectives on church and ministry most effectively renew organizations that are flexible and committed to the process for the long haul. Grenz believes the congregations and judicatories that most successfully adapt church structures to emergent theology and ministry are those that successfully develop an attitude that says, "We'll try it, and if it doesn't work, we'll try something else," instead of, "But we've always done it this way." Adopting practices of making decisions fairly quickly, trying things out, and being willing to jettison whatever doesn't work without blaming or complaining are important qualities. Perhaps most important, at all levels of the church and ministry, is the authenticity of the spiritual life of the organization. "Making God's presence more obvious and expressing gratitude for all God has given us, as well as a 'sense of thankfulness for abundance' rather than complaining about 'what is lacking' makes a huge difference!"[32]

DEEP CHANGE OR SLOW DEATH

One of the historical realities about baptism that has largely been lost is the connection between baptism and death. Through our baptism we are united with Christ in his death *and* in his resurrection, "so we too might walk in newness of life" (Rom. 6:4-5). Andy Crouch writes that baptism had not only deeply shaped the self-understanding of the early church but that the connection between baptism and death was also concrete to them. The early Christians of the Pauline era "had the experience of being plunged underwater, metaphorically buried and placed in a grave, then raised up from that watery grave by another's hand. Their bodies carry the memory of that death and resurrection."[33]

In Christian life, death and resurrection are linked, and thus one needs to go through the process of dying literally or figuratively in order to be born anew. Robin Greenwood suggests that developing the ministry of the baptized is to encourage people in congregations to recognize that change is a normal part of life, and that we need not panic. "The assumption may be that if numbers are in decline, the leadership ineffective or the roof insecure, God has abandoned us. Yet the challenge to Christians in any age is to recognize that the coming reign of God is not to be equated with our preferred or inherited patterns of church life. God is as much in the dying of particular forms of church as in regeneration. Letting go of the panicked attempt to sustain particular forms at all costs is being prepared to lose our lives for the sake of the gospel."[34]

How this regeneration is lived out varies from person to person and congregation to congregation. For ourselves and for our churches, we must die to that which is no longer life giving. It can be difficult to remember in North America that for Christians in the ancient world, as well as Christians in our world today, the association of baptism with death has a literal connotation, and that the biblical image of being "crucified with Christ" is not simply a metaphor, but for many a lived experience. "I have been crucified with Christ; and it is no longer I who live, but it is Christ who lives in me" (Gal. 2:19-20).

Carolyn Jourdan, in *Heart in the Right Place*, tells of her transformation from life as an attorney on Capitol Hill in Washington to new life as a receptionist in her father's medical office in the Tennessee mountains after her mother had a heart attack. She shares a story that illustrates the connections between baptism, death, and new life. Jourdan accompanies her friend Henry, who operates the heart-lung machine at the local hospital, to watch an open-heart surgery. At one point in the story, Henry stops the heart of the woman on the operating table. A devout mystic and participant in baptismal living, Henry explains to Carolyn that she did not need to be fearful, and that what she was seeing was a form of initiation rite, or a "medical sacrament":

> [Henry says] "Well, what we're doing is taking a person who's your everyday kind of flawed normal mortal and giving them an experience of the afterlife, a taste of God, and then bringing them back into the world. It usually changes them forever."
>
> I stared at him dumbfounded.
>
> He continued. "It's like what John the Baptist did to Jesus when we baptized him in the river Jordan. The real meaning of that's gotten lost over time. What people don't understand anymore is that John just didn't dunk Jesus. He held him under the water until he pretty well drowned him. He gave him a near death experience, so when he came back he'd bring back a vision of Heaven with him. That fellow that came back wasn't just a human man, Jesus, anymore, but something more; he was the Christ. . . ."
>
> "Well, no wonder my baptism didn't feel like anything," [Carolyn] said. "They just immersed me." I just thought more about what Henry had told me. "I heard that big operations like this changed people, but I thought it was fear causing the change. Facing their own mortality."
>
> "Well, it's not," [said Henry]. "Seeing God is what causes it. Facing their immortality."
>
> Wow.[35]

For small congregations the ministry of the baptized brings many challenges, including the need to die to previously held images and ideas of what the church is and should be in order to bring about resurrection. Robert E. Quinn, professor of organizational behavior and human resources at the Graduate School of Business, University of Michigan, Ann Arbor, writes that leaders who want to make a difference in organizations today are embedded in a dilemma. That is, we must continually choose between *deep change* or *slow death*. Change is everywhere, Quinn believes,

and while this has always been the case, the need for deep change in organizations is more blatant than ever. "We are all regularly lured into play-
ing the role of the powerless victim or the passive observer," he writes.
"To choose to play either of these roles is to choose meaninglessness of
the self or the slow death of self." Quinn argues that while choosing to
undergo deep personal and organizational change is difficult, the transformation that ensues encourages others to undergo a similar experience:

> We are all potential change agents. As we discipline our talents, we deepen our
> perception of what is possible. We develop a reverence for the tools and the
> relationships that surround us. We then bring a discipline to our visions and
> grow in integrity. Life becomes more meaningful. We become empowered and
> empowering to our context. Having experienced deep change in ourselves, we are
> able to bring deep change to the systems around us.[36]

Robin Greenwood and Hugh Burgess, in their book *Power: Changing Society and the Churches*, link change agents in the church today with biblical
prophets: "Change agents in the Church, like prophets, review and challenge the way things are. . . . True prophets of every age, reluctantly, have
received their message as a hot burning coal from the altar of deep worship and love for God."[37] Greenwood and Burgess stress that much like
the ancient prophets, contemporary change agents also "paint pictures"
through visions and story to demonstrate new life. At the same time,
change agents in the church need the skills to turn ideas into action. On
a concrete level, this means nurture, education, spiritual resources, and
encouragement for everyone to work it out together.[38]

Through his work on deep change, Quinn has developed a tool
called "the transformational cycle." The cycle depicts transformation as
a dynamic process. Organizations that see themselves within the cycle,
such as congregations, are also dynamic. In the context of transformation, leadership involves risk taking, learning, and change. Such leaders need to have faith, embrace ambiguity, and build trust. While these
concepts are not commonly associated with the business organizations
that Quinn typically examines, they are familiar concepts in churches
and religious organizations. Part of the challenge in congregations may
be that we have looked at these concepts and ourselves too superfi-

cially. We have acculturated a sense that our small congregations have little potential, and we have lost reverence for our ministries. Perhaps we have adopted attitudes of detachment, reconciling ourselves to the slow death of our churches. In his work, Quinn recalls how some Ford Motor Company managers attained one of the highest awards in their field by concluding that risk taking and learning precipitate any transformation, and that deep change is necessary to maintain excellence in organizations. These important findings echo baptismal theology and ministry profoundly and support the belief that God has given the church the gifts we need for ministry.[39]

The transformational cycle assumes that every system, every organization, every congregation, is continuously evolving. The cycle has four distinct phases: initiation, uncertainty, transformational, and routinization. As a dynamic evolutionary process, the transformational cycle is

Figure 4.1. The Transformational Cycle.
From Robert E. Quinn, *Deep Change: Discovering the Leader Within*, 168. Copyright 1996, Jossey-Bass. Reprinted with permission of John Wiley and Sons, Inc.

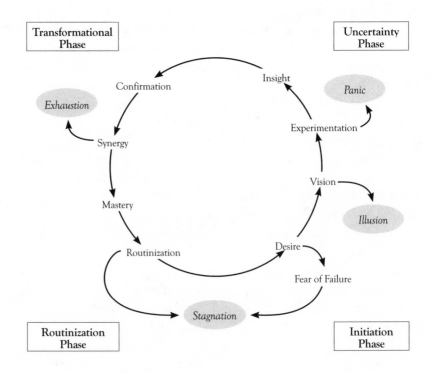

rooted in relationships; the stages are in relationship to each other. Individuals are in their own transformational cycles, and those relate to the transformational cycle of the whole congregation. For an organization or congregation to remain vital, it must continuously cycle through all four stages of growth and expansion, or fall into decay. It is not easy to keep the transformational cycle moving. There are four traps into which individuals or congregations may fall along the way: illusion, panic, exhaustion, and stagnation. Detours into any of these traps can lead to stagnation, decay, even a fast death for congregations. One of the major ways small congregations fall out of the cycle of transformation is to pursue, consciously or unconsciously, a strategy of incremental investment. There is simply no way that transformation, as a dynamic and evolutionary process, can be reduced to partial transformation or be completed by following a checklist. As in baptism, we are called to offer all we are and all we have to the process, without holding back parts of ourselves out of fear or panic. Along the way, the promise of resurrection is both a sign and a guide to what is promised.[40]

Each of the four phases of the transformational cycle holds the potential for both promise and challenge for members of small congregations as individuals and collectively. Below is an explanation of the four phases adapted to baptismal ministry and small congregations:

INITIATION

An iteration of the transformational cycle occurs whenever an individual or a group within a congregation seeks growth and renewal. Ongoing learning and reflection precede the initiation phase. Through discernment, a vision is shaped and then the person or group begins to take risks and reimagine the future.

UNCERTAINTY

At this phase there is usually some uncertainty about whether or not a vision is realistic or illusory. There is a significant danger for congregations in the initiation phase to become invested in a vision that cannot be implemented. Congregations caught in the trap of illusion and unable to let go of an unrealistic vision are practicing self-deception. To stay out of the trap of illusion, congregations must negotiate movement to the uncertainty phase through active experimentation, albeit with an uncertain outcome. For instance, commitment to a plan of study for adult formation, or implementing new hospitality practices, or discerning shared ministries are all characteristics of active experimentations. At this phase, the outcome of any of these actions is not clear, but the experimenting allows members of the congregation to try on the vision, perhaps receive a glimpse of the promise to come. If the congregation is unable to cope with the uncertainty of experimentation, or if the experiments appear to fail, the congregation could fall into another trap, or a state of panic. If the congregation can resist becoming paralyzed by panic, and instead remain engaged in experimentation by reframing problems into opportunities for further learning, new insights and new paradigms may emerge from lived experience.

TRANSFORMATIONAL

The transformational phase of the cycle is the essence of deep change. In this phase congregations live into the new paradigm of baptismal ministry and have the skills to reframe contradictory elements toward transformation. In the transformational phase, there is not only a new vision but also a new life resultant from all the study, formation, and experimentation the congregation has experienced. The energy in the congregational system, including individuals and the group as a whole, is palpable and results in synergy. Given that baptismal ministry is rooted in relationship, the relationships among the members of a congregation are transformed by the process as well and are generally healthy and authentic. The trap at this stage of the cycle is for the congregation, particularly those who have emerged as leaders in the process, to collapse into exhaustion. Instead of falling into this trap, leaders need to invite others into the circle in an effort to maintain a genuine shared leadership model.

ROUTINIZATION

Instead of a collapse into exhaustion, the congregation remains in the transformational cycle by maintaining the new vision through more stable routines. The trap for congregations in this phase is stagnation, when baptismal ministry becomes "This is the way we have always done it." For congregations, stagnation easily leads to slow death. Instead, congregations continue on the transformational cycle through ongoing evaluation, re-visioning, and realignment of the church and ministry.[41]

The design of the transformational cycle itself presents an interesting exercise for groups within congregations. They might ask: where do we see ourselves on the transformational cycle at this point in our congregational life? Where are our opportunities for deep change, here and now? What are the potential traps challenging our congregation? Although there is not one way for a congregation to pursue transformation, the transformational cycle is a tool to help with the process.

BAPTISMAL ECCLESIOLOGY AND THEOLOGICAL EDUCATION

Changing perspectives on the church and ministry directly affect theological education. Peyton G. Craighill, of the Church of the Redeemer in Bryn Mawr, Pennsylvania, in a 2007 paper on seminary education written for the Ministry Developers Collaborative, makes a plea for models of theological education that prepare students "to promote ministry as the mission of all baptized people in all aspects of daily life." He believes that such theological education calls for seminaries to "face the challenge of a renewed vision of ministry" and rethink their mission:

> No longer is it enough to teach students how to *do* ministry themselves. They must learn how to *share* ministry by helping others to live into the ministries that Christ, through their baptismal covenant, calls them to. As students come to seminary, they should be helped to recognize that they are not just preparing *for* ministry. Through their baptism, they have already been *in* ministry for many years.[42]

Louis Weil believes that if theological education is to serve the whole church, then it must be intentionally grounded in baptismal ecclesiology. As someone who taught in seminaries for more than forty years, Weil knows that theological education has an integral if not expanded role to play in the education and formation of the whole people of God. "Tragically, however, such training often confirms candidates in the highly clericalized understanding of the Church's life they often bring with them from their own parish experience."[43]

"I am convinced that we will need all the seminary graduates we can produce in the coming years," writes Katharine Jefferts Schori, the presiding bishop of the Episcopal Church. "But they will need to be formed and deployed differently." Jefferts Schori sees that there are lots of opportunities for ministry, for the baptized to use their gifts, and a diminishing number of congregations that can afford full-time, paid seminary clergy, even if that were the primary agenda of the church. Jefferts Schori believes that leadership development for the baptized is the key to the church of the future. "We need leaders in the church—and I insist that every baptized person is a Christian leader somewhere—who knows how to lay down their lives. . . . We don't need prima donnas, who need to be the center of ecclesiastical attention. The last time I checked, the body of Christ already had a head, and it's not you or me or the rector down the street."[44]

If the church begins to recognize that the authority for ministry begins at baptism rather than at ordination, then theological education is charged not only with preparing people for preaching, teaching, and pastoral care but also with skills for supporting all members for their ministries. "For years seminaries have been talking about working more directly on the local level. The question was always 'how?'" says Steven Charleston, former dean and president of EDS and assisting bishop in the Diocese of California. "If the role of theological education is to empower ministers to carry out the gospel, and the mission of the church is to embody that gospel in the world, then we must unite these two dynamics. The gospel is both empowered and embodied like never before."[45]

DISCUSSION QUESTIONS

Try this reflection exercise with members of your congregation:

In silence, imagine visiting your congregation as a seeker on a typical Sunday morning. You have no previous experience of the congregation and are new to the community. Imagine walking through the front door on that first Sunday in the congregation, and reflect on your experience of the worship, education, hospitality, or whatever is typical. Try to engage your imagination through all your senses—what do you see, hear, smell, touch, feel? Write down your initial impressions and then share what you experienced with others from your congregation. Try not to judge or problem-solve, rather share your experience as a speaker.

Finally, reflect as a group on the following questions:

1. Based on a typical Sunday morning in your congregation, what does the experience tell you about your theology of the church, or ecclesiology, and ministry? What is the church? Who are the ministers? How is it evident to a seeker that your congregation bears witness to the gospel?

2. As you reflect on your congregation, when has its life been the most vibrant, most welcoming?

3. Where do you experience discontinuities between the ministry and mission, or your congregation and its organization?

4. What is the relationship between what happens on Sunday in your congregation and the ministry of the whole people of God on Monday? How is this connection apparent?

5. If a seeker visited your congregation on a typical Sunday, what would the experience tell them about the priorities of that community?

BEST PRACTICES FOR BAPTISMAL MINISTRY DEVELOPMENT

T his is something I have found to be true without exception: that when we, any of us, focus on things in our lives that are passing away, we get scared, we get anxious, we get depressed, we lose hope; and when we focus on things that are being birthed and are coming newly into creation, we get excited, we get imaginative, we get optimistic, we feel drawn closer to one another, we feel as if we have meaning and purpose in this life, and we have joy. . . . It's about keeping our focus upon God's Dream. And the wonders and miracles. My friends, you know, we are given change as an ingredient in life. We can be frightened and anxious and resistant to it or we can embrace it as a tool to transform us.[1]

—JIM KELSEY (1952–2007)

When Jim Kelsey, the bishop of the Episcopal Diocese of Northern Michigan spoke these words at his last diocesan convention in 2007, he was commenting on institutional change and its impact on congregations and judicatories. Many places throughout the Christian church are faced with hard realities such as declining membership and financial shortages. "The way we have always done it before" was never realistic for those locations challenged by geography, poverty, and low population, and it is becoming increasingly unrealistic for other, more prosperous and populous regions. The need for systemic change throughout mainline denominations has been verified through a number of studies as well as the experience of congregational members themselves. Jim Kelsey believed that the task at hand is "a matter of letting go of the familiar and being opened to new life—new surprise—new birth which God does have in store for us."[2] Throughout this book are examples of congregations and judicatories that have faithfully embraced change and experienced transformation through baptismal ministry. These changes do not necessarily eradicate all the challenges to be faced, but individuals and communities are transformed by the journey, and through clarity of purpose and mutual responsibility new life is found. The congregations and judicatories transformed through baptismal ministry development look beyond survival to embrace the future with a sense of hope and abundance.

This book, *Born of Water, Born of Spirit*, was part of our ongoing reflection on the experience of the Pastoral Excellence Project of EDS in Cambridge, Massachusetts, working in partnership with the dioceses of northern New England—Maine, New Hampshire, and Vermont—and beyond, in areas such as Northern Michigan, Wyoming, and Scotland, to support pastoral leaders in small rural congregations. The project sought to nurture, sustain, train, and educate pastoral leaders in regions traditionally neglected by denominations and seminaries, where few full-time pastors are sustained locally and where everyone working to build the life of church communities is challenged by limited resources spread over vast geographical areas. In these contexts, affirming the ministry of the baptized within congregations not only stretches limited resources, it also revitalizes congregations through a renewed sense of abundance and pastoral excellence. Pastoral leaders in these communities move from the traditional sense of congregations gathered around a minister to new life as gathered ministering communities that value the gifts and skills for ministry of all the baptized. The one question that baptismal ministry development attempts to answer, according to Manuel Padilla, ministry developer in the Diocese of Northern Michigan, is "How do we form our members to be an effective Christian witness in their context?"[3]

Throughout this project, pastoral leaders identified several factors associated with a renewed emphasis on the ministry of the baptized in small rural congregations, including the following:

- Generosity of spirit rooted in a theology of abundance
- Openness to creativity and new experience
- Commitment to the ministry of every member
- Intentional hospitality—opening the doors to the community
- Immersion in prayer and worship
- Emphasis on small groups for study and nurture
- Intergenerational participation in all aspects of community life
- Reconciliation and healing within the community
- Shared leadership and decision making
- Commitment to social justice through outreach and service
- Ecumenical and interfaith partnerships
- Expansive denominational identity
- Ecological consciousness through the care of resources, stewardship, and the environment

Since congregations are rooted in their local context, a single recipe for baptismal ministry development cannot be formulated. A commitment to baptismal ministry can be found in congregations of all sizes and at all economic levels; what is critical is that the congregation sees the recovery of the priesthood of all believers as integral to the transformation of the church and ministry and therefore in its own self-interest.

While the focus of this book is small congregations, often in remote and underserved regions, it is clear that baptismal ministry development is a resource to support vitality in other congregations as well. As the stories featured in this book suggest, each congregation and judicatory has been transformed through baptismal ministry development, yet each has had its own affirmations and issues along the way, and each has different challenges to face in the future. Although each congregation and judicatory featured here has grown as a result of baptismal ministry development, also clear is that for each of these congregations growth means more than an increased number of members. To be sure, some of the congregations featured here have experienced numerical growth, although in many cases the increase in membership is modest compared to the spiritual growth gained, or the growth in community involvement shared by the congregation, or even the growth in relationships between members. Within baptismal ministry development, congregational growth is not exclusively limited to numbers; spiritual growth, growth in commitment, growth in community involvement, and growth in relationships are equally important growth factors.

Best Practices for Baptismal Ministry Development

Without ignoring the distinctiveness of each congregation and judicatory, it is possible to suggest some of the best practices of baptismal ministry development that are evident in the stories told in this book and applicable in other contexts.

1.   Congregations *build on health*, where

   •   people interact with each other in respectful and appropriate ways,
   •   a sense of trust pervades relationships,
   •   feelings and ideas are expressed directly and openly,
   •   gifts of all are welcomed and used appropriately,
   •   clergy and laity use power justly and constructively for the common good and recognize the abuse of power,
   •   community is formed intentionally, before leaders are identified,
   •   an openness to ongoing education and issues is evident in the community,
   •   spiritual concerns and pastoral care of members are addressed,
   •   practical realities are assessed and addressed, people have an opportunity to know and experience their power together.

2.   *They know their history and listen to stories*—the heritage and traditions that influence mission and ministry—and they understand their interpretation both from the perspective of inherited models of the church and ministry and from baptismal ministry development. If a congregation is destined to be something more

than a museum, attention to the stories of spiritual ancestors and current members is a means of transforming where they have been and where they wish to go. How does the history shape perceptions of mission and ministry? To facilitate transformation, negative history must be confronted and addressed directly. Deep listening to the stories of the people reveals their hopes, dreams, and aspirations for the future.

3. *They invite all to share their gifts for ministry.* Their leaders believe that everybody has gifts for ministry, understand the need for a paradigm shift, are committed to change, view baptismal ministry development as *process* more than product or program, and experience a call to transformation—recognizing the risks inherent in this work and the various forms of resistance they may encounter. A key paradigm shift is the understanding that ministry is communal rather than individual, as is the belief that God gives each congregation all the gifts needed for a vital ministry. Further, such congregations recognize and practice ministry as a dynamic *partnership* rather than ascribe to models based on control or domination.

4. *They commit to learning in community.* Ongoing spiritual formation for all ages is a priority and an attitude of constant learning pervades the congregation. Although a variety of resources are available to support the ministry of the baptized in congregations, they all hold in common the desire to embrace and nurture the giftedness of all God's people as well as the belief in the sacredness of all creation. In baptismal ministry development, learning is holistic; that is, it encompasses all of life, not only those parts formally associated with the church. We are all teachers and learners, and ministry includes the personal, the communal, the neighborhood, and the wider world. Learning in community often begins with questions, not answers, and requires evolving leadership roles and new skills.

5. *They share a rich symbolic life*—expressed in worship, music, education, governance, pastoral care, outreach, even architecture (seating, windows, art)—to reflect the many ways God is present throughout community. A central theme of the rich symbolic life

of baptismal ministry development is the theme of *abundance* and the belief that the Spirit has many expressions and is never exhausted by one expression. Theological themes such as death and resurrection, the body of Christ, commissioning, and the reign of God are also an important part of symbolic life. The shift from thinking in terms of scarcity to living into abundance has an impact on all areas of common life and is integral to a congregation's sense of hope for the future. Congregations practicing baptismal ministry development reflect on ancient symbols of faith, often interpreting them in new and contextual ways. The various callings of the community are celebrated in worship and ministry.

6. *They develop wider community, denominational and ecumenical relationships* that support baptismal ministry. Such congregations discern ministry priorities locally and actively seek partners willing to work for the common good. They move away from framing relationships hierarchically and toward a spirit of mutual responsibility. In baptismal ministry development collaboration is a positive force for good and manifests the creativity of the Spirit. Through our baptism, Christians make a commitment to work toward God's dream for all humankind and all of creation, not limited to other Christians. Congregations committed to baptismal ministry development seek denominational partnerships and encourage dialogue on changing perspectives on the church and ministry.

7. *They implement ongoing discernment evaluation* and realize that baptismal ministry development is a long-term commitment. Without ongoing and intentional discernment and evaluation, any congregation will lose its relevance, energy, or direction. Congregations practicing baptismal ministry development realize the importance of self-awareness and cultivate regular practices to assess where they are and consciously work toward raising up succeeding generations.

8. *They cultivate a life of prayer and spiritual stamina.* God calls all humankind to a life of deep abundance. Our spirituality reflects the relationships we have with God, other people, and the world. Scripture portrays Jesus as constantly crossing cultural boundaries. Baptismal ministry development is countercultural in that it challenges inherited assumptions about rugged individualism

and consumer-based ministry delivery systems. A disciplined life of prayer and reflection is perhaps the greatest source of support for congregations choosing to develop the ministry of the baptized. Baptismal ministry development is, ultimately, a spiritual journey, an invitation for people in community to awaken to God in all creation and to rediscover whose we are. Learning new skills is important but not enough. Rather, baptismal ministry development calls us to rediscover our center and to awaken to the Spirit everywhere.[4]

CHALLENGES FOR THEOLOGICAL EDUCATION

For many of the pastoral leaders who participated in the Pastoral Excellence Project at EDS, it was their first formal seminary experience. For others, the project was their first experience of a seminary that took seriously the challenges they face in poor and sometimes remote areas. Because of the project, EDS has also changed; it is more committed than ever to preparing students for ministries in nontraditional settings. Already our classrooms have changed through the use of innovative educational technologies and the production of ministry development courses especially geared for students in small rural congregations.

Baptismal ministry development seriously challenges theological education. It suggests the need for educational models that are accessible to a wider audience of pastoral leaders than traditional and expensive residential seminary degrees. Congregations interested in exploring baptismal ministry often cite the need for more education and training. When theological schools take baptismal ministry seriously, theological education will be more grounded, locally astute, culturally diverse, and technologically accessible. The key challenge for judicatories, seminaries, and theological schools is to continue to develop educational resources and training models for pastoral leaders in these abundant communities of faith.

The late Wes Frensdorff, one of the major advocates of baptismal ministry development in North America, argued that the primary purpose of all religious education should be the spiritual formation of the baptized for living out their baptismal vows, rather than primarily focused on educating ordination candidates. While the current educational process for mainline denominations flows from a particular candidate's sense of call, to education and discernment, to ordination, to ministry, Frensdorff advocated formation that begins with ministry and education in community, then call and discernment, followed by ordination and ongoing education and ministry. "Perhaps then we would find theological education in pursuit of a broader agenda, while still concerned with preserving and proclaiming the memory of who we have been as a church. We might also be concerned with who we and the world for which Christ died are becoming."[5]

As the people of God, the priesthood of all believers, we are called to respond to a world that craves healing and wholeness. As the Christian church, our interdependence is intended to be a source of strength and a gift from God. As people of faith, we know that the reign of God will be built on the transformation of hearts—on *new* life, not just reordered life. Through the recovery of the authority for ministry given at our baptism, we can face the challenges to the religious institutions of our day, transforming our structures and awakening our spirits to the God in our midst. We are all called to transform the church and ministry to better respond to the joys and the challenges of our increasingly diverse world. The future of the church depends on it.

Discussion Questions

1. Reflect on the image of the *dream of God* mentioned in the opening quotation. What is the dream of God for your congregation?

2. How does your congregation need to change to live into the dream?

3. Reflect on the image of *journey*. How have you experienced your own spiritual journey and the journey of your congregation? What other images of the church and ministry do you carry forward from this book?

4. In baptismal ministry development, partnerships are key. Where are the opportunities for partnership for your congregation?

5. What are the thoughts and feelings that you take home as you read this book?

NOTES

INTRODUCTION

1. David Roozen, "Faith Communities Today," in *American Congregations*, Hartford Institute for Religious Research (Hartford: Hartford Seminary, 2007), 4-9. Throughout this study the term *oldline* is used instead of the more common *mainline*, referring to the oldest Protestant denominations historically: American Baptist, Disciples of Christ, Episcopal, Evangelical Lutheran Church in America, Presbyterian (USA), Reformed Church in America, United Church of Christ, and Unitarian Universalism.

2. Robert E. Quinn, *Deep Change: Discovering the Leader Within* (San Francisco: Jossey-Bass, 1996).

3. "The Use of the Means of Grace: A Statement on the Promise of Word and Sacrament," Evangelical Lutheran Church in America, 1997. See "Baptism (Lutheran View)," ELCA website, www.elca.org.

4. John Calvin, *Institutes of the Christian Religion*, (London: Arnold Hatfield for Bonham Norton, 1599), bk. 4, chap. 15, sec. 1; Center for Reformed Theology and Politics website, http://www.reformed.org/master/index.html?mainframe=/books/institutes/.

5. A. Theodore Eastman, "Holy and Creative Spirit," 1975, rev. 2009.

6. William Stringfellow, "The Liturgy as Political Event, The Political Authority of Baptism," in *Documents of Witness: A History of the Episcopal Church, 1782-1985*, ed. Don S. Armentrout and Robert Boak Slocum (New York: Church Hymnal, 1994), 550-51.

7. Herbert Anderson and Edward Foley, *Mighty Stories, Dangerous Rituals: Weaving Together the Human and the Divine* (San Francisco: Jossey-Bass, 1998), 70.

8. "What Is the Ecclesiology of Local Collaborative Ministry? A Summary of the Foundational Theology and the Four Marks," Scottish Episcopal Church, October 7, 2006.

9. See, for example, Moltmann's autobiographical note on the development of his theology of hope in A. J. Conyers, *God, Hope, and History: Jurgen Moltmann and the Christian Concept of History* (Macon, GA: Mercer University Press, 1988), 203-23; and Elie Wiesel, *After the Darkness: Reflections on the Holocaust*, trans. Benjamin Moser (New York: Schocken Books, 2002).

10. See Michael J. McClymond, "Making Sense of the Census, or, What 1,999,563,838

Christians Might Mean for the Study of Religion," *Journal of the American Academy of Religion* (December 2002): 884–85, with statistics drawn from the *World Christian Encyclopedia* (New York: Oxford University Press, 2001); and Donald E. Miller, "April Is The Cruelest Month," *Sightings*, May 2, 2003.

11. Louis Weil, *A Theology of Worship* (Cambridge, MA: Cowley Publications, 2002), 127.

12. Definitions are a composite of working definitions from a variety of sources, including the Episcopal dioceses of Vermont, Northern Michigan, and Northern California; New Song Episcopal Church; the Total Ministry website, www.totalministry.org; and the Ministry Developers Collaborative.

13. "About Baptismal Living and Ministry" (paper, Episcopal Diocese of Vermont, 2007).

14. Verna J. Dozier, *The Dream of God: A Call to Return* (Cambridge, MA: Cowley, 1991), 142.

15. Definition for *ministry development* is from Manuel Padilla of the Episcopal Diocese of Northern Michigan, April 2009.

16. See the website of the Episcopal Diocese of Northern California under "Total Ministry" for this definition and the nine principles, www.dncweb.org.

17. Thomas Clark Ely, "Wade in the Water," diocesan convention address, Burlington, Vermont, November 15, 2002.

18. Ibid.

19. See "About the Disciples," "Baptism" at the Christian Church (Disciples of Christ) website, www.disciples.org.

20. "The Use of the Means of Grace: A Statement on the Promise of Word and Sacrament," Evangelical Lutheran Church in America, 1997; "Baptism (Lutheran View)," ELCA website, www.elca.org.

21. Mark C. Trotter, pastor of First United Methodist Church in San Diego, California, quoted in "A United Methodist Understanding of Baptism," Temecula United Methodist, Temecula, CA, website, www.temeculaumc.com/baptism.cfm.

22. Christopher L. Webber, *A User's Guide to Morning Prayer and Baptism* (Harrisburg, PA: Morehouse Publishing, 1997), 37.

23. Ian T. Douglas, "Baptized into Mission: Ministry and Holy Orders Reconsidered," *Sewanee Theological Review* 40, no. 4 (1997): 435–36.

24. Klara Tammany, *Living Water: Baptism as a Way of Life* (New York: Church Publishing, 2002).

25. Deborah Flemister Mullen, "Baptism as Sacrament of Struggle and Rite of Resistance," in *Ending Racism in the Church*, ed. Susan E. Davies and Sister Paul Teresa Hennessee (Cleveland: United Church Press, 1998), 66–73.

26. Walter Brueggemann, *Hope within History* (Atlanta: John Knox Press, 1987), 87. Brueggemann's insights have repeatedly guided this introduction.

27. Daniel J. Harrington, *The Church According to the New Testament: What the Wisdom and Witness of Early Christianity Teach Us Today* (Franklin, WI: Sheed & Ward, 2001), 74.

28. Sara Maitland, *A Big-Enough God: A Feminist's Search for a Joyful Theology* (New York: Riverhead Books, 1995), 167.

29. *The Calling of the Laity: Verna Dozier's Anthology* (Herndon, VA: Alban Institute, 1988), 115.

30. "Baptism: A Practice of Faith in the United Church of Christ," at the United Church of Christ website, "About Baptism," www.ucc.org/worship/baptism/.

31. See also Brueggemann, *Hope within History*, 3, 68.

32. Maitland, *Big-Enough God*, 167.

33. Cited in Vincent Harding, *Hope and History: Why We Must Share the Story of the Movement* (Maryknoll, NY: Orbis Books, 1990), 212.

34. Quoted in *Yes!* 24 (Winter 2003); see also Harding, "Letter to Teachers in Religious Communities and Institutions," *Hope and History*, 201–28.

35. "Use of the Means of Grace," principle 14.

36. I (Fredrica) owe this observation to my faculty colleague and Massachusetts state representative, Byron Rushing.

37. Verna J. Dozier, *The Dream of God: A Call to Return* (Cambridge, MA: Cowley, 1991), 142.

38. Philip W. Butin, "What Presbyterians Believe: Baptism," *Presbyterian Survey*, June 1995, www.pcusa.org.

39. Katharine Jefferts Schori, letter to the people of the Diocese of San Joaquin, *The Redwood Log*, http://stjohnslakeportparish.googlepages.com/theecho.

40. From the 1662 *Book of Common Prayer*. Interesting is that the 1979 Prayer Book substitutes *refuge* for *hope*.

41. Brueggemann, *Hope within History*, 69, 80.

42. James C. Fenhagen, *Mutual Ministry: New Vitality for the Local Church* (New York: Seabury Press, 1977), 141.

CHAPTER 1

1. For example, see "Expanding Mission and Vitality in Small Congregations: A Framework for Affirming and Strengthening the Ministry of Small Churches" (report, Standing Commission of the Church in Small Communities, The Episcopal Church, 2003); see also, report of the Standing Commission for Small Congregations, 2006.

2. Bob Honeychurch, "Small-Membership Church," The Episcopal Church, http://www.episcopalchurch.org/smallchurch.html.

3. Samuel J. Wylie, *The Celebration of Smallness*, 2nd ed. (Marquette, MI: Diocese of Northern Michigan, 1995), 6–8.

4. Elaine Cameron, "Theological Education with the Laity: The Study of One Congregation's Experience of Local Collaborative Ministry" (DMin thesis, Pittsburgh Theological Seminary, May 2006).

5. For a larger discussion, see the Web page "Understanding Small Church Dynamics," at the Episcopal Church website, http://www.episcopalchurch.org/smallchurch_5234_ENG_HTM.htm.

6. *EDS News* (Spring 2002), 6.

7. Ibid.

8. Kevin Cross, letters to Sheryl Kujawa-Holbrook, December 2009; January 2009.

9. Also see Andy McKeever, "Attracting Newcomers," *Bennington Banner*, May 12, 2008.

10. Kortright Davis, *Serving with Power: Reviving the Spirit of Christian Ministry* (New York: Paulist Press, 1999), 145.

11. Anthony B. Robinson, *Transforming Congregational Culture* (Grand Rapids: Eerdmans, 2003), 35–38.

12. Willa Goodfellow, interview with Sheryl Kujawa-Holbrook, March 19, 2009.

13. James Kelsey, interview with Sheryl Kujawa-Holbrook, October 2006.

14. Ibid.

15. Lance R. Barker and B. Edmon Martin, eds., *Multiple Paths to Ministry: New Models for Theological Education* (Cleveland: Pilgrim Press, 2004), 38.

16. Ibid., 40.

17. Kelsey, interview.

18. Christianne Humphrey, letter to Fredrica Harris Thompsett, June 20, 2007.

19. Steven Croft, *Transforming Communities: Re-imagining the Church for the 21st Century* (London: Darton, Longman and Todd, 2002), 73.

20. Ibid., 71.

21. Adapted from "Expanding Mission and Vitality in Small Congregations," 2003.

22. See also "Total Ministry" website, http://totalministry.org.

23. Details about the Redwood Episcopal Cluster may be found at the Episcopal Diocese of Northern California website, http://stfranciswillits.org/missioner.aspx.

24. St. Francis in the Redwoods congregational profile, Episcopal Diocese of Northern California website, http://stfranciswillits.org.

25. Josephine Borgeson, interview with Sheryl Kujawa-Holbrook, March 2009.

26. For the testimony and information on the congregations in the Redwood Episcopal Cluster, see "About Total Ministry," at http://stfranciswillits.org/totalministry.aspx.

27. Daniel P. Smith and Mary K. Sellon, *Pathway to Renewal: Practical Steps for Congregations* (Herndon, VA: Alban Institute, 2008), 6.

CHAPTER 2

1. For an overview of the history and organization of the Border Parish, see Carole Wageman, "Report on Baptismal Ministry in Vermont," May 2003, 20–24.

2. James C. Fenhagen, *Mutual Ministry: New Vitality for the Local Church* (New York: Seabury, 1977), 26.

3. Ibid., 26–30.

4. Adapted from Fenhagen, *Mutual Ministry*, 28–29.

5. Marianne H. Micks, *Deep Waters: An Introduction to Baptism* (Cambridge, MA: Cowley Publications, 1996), 42.

6. Ibid., 93.

7. Daniel B. Stevick, "Holy Baptism," Supplement to *Prayer Book Studies* 26 (New York: Church Hymnal Corporation, 1973), 88–89.

8. "Theology of LSM," Anglican Diocese of Auckland, www.auckanglican.org. nz/?sid:20 (accessed February 2009). Terms have been adjusted to be more inclusive of non-Anglicans.

9. Andrew McGowan, "Living and Proclaiming the Baptismal Covenant," lecture, the Episcopal Divinity School, May 1999.

10. Ibid.

11. Ibid.

12. Wesley Frensdorff, "The Captivity of Sacraments," *The Witness*, April 1992, 5.

13. Kevin L. Thew Forrester, *"I Have Called You Friends . . .": An Invitation to Ministry* (New York: Church Publishing, 2003), viii.

14. Ibid.

15. Nancy Moore, interview with Sheryl Kujawa-Holbrook, January 2006.

16. Chilton Knudsen, interview with Sheryl Kujawa-Holbrook, January 2006.

17. See Robin Greenwood, *Transforming Church: Liberating Structures for Ministry* (London: SPCK, 2002), chap. 4.

18. Moore, interview.

19. See the document, "Immanuel Parish. A Brief History of the Covenant Group/Ministry Support Team: How We Got to Where We Are" (Immanuel Church, Bellows Falls, VT, n.d.). For a synopsis of the history of Immanuel Church in regard to baptismal ministry, see Wageman, "Report on Baptismal Ministry in Vermont," 12–18.

20. "Immanuel Parish. Brief History of the Covenant Group."

21. Wageman, "Report on Baptismal Ministry in Vermont," 14.

22. Ibid.

23. David Bateman, "St. Thaddaeus' Parish Welcomes Shared Ministry," *The East Tennessee Episcopalian*, April/May 2006; also, Bateman, "Ministry Development Assignment Evolving, Govan Says," *The East Tennessee Episcopalian*, June/July 2005.

24. Carter Paden, "Chattanooga Rector Relates Parish's Experience with Shared Ministry," *The East Tennessee Episcopalian*, June/July 2007.

25. Joani Koch, letter to Sheryl Kujawa-Holbrook, March 25, 2009.

26. Elaine Cameron, "Theological Education with the Laity: The Study of One Congregation's Experience of Local Collaborative Ministry" (DMin thesis, Pittsburgh Theological Seminary, May 2006).

27. Wageman, "Report on Baptismal Ministry in Vermont," 17.

28. Developed by the Ministry Support Team, the Diocese of Vermont.

29. Greenwood, *Transforming Church*, 81.

30. Ibid., 83.

31. Ibid.

32. Jenny Joyce, letter to Kevin Thew Forrester, July 19, 2006.

33. R. Paul Stevens, quoted in Joyce, letter to Kevin Thew Forrester, July 19, 2006.

34. Thomas Ray, "The Small Church: Radical Reformation and Renewal of Ministry," in Lance R. Barker and B. Edmon Martin, eds., *Multiple Paths to Ministry: New Models for Theological Education* (Cleveland: Pilgrim Press, 2004), 161.

35. Ray, "The Small Church," in Barker and Martin, *Multiple Paths to Ministry*, 164–67; 169–70.

36. Ibid., 167–68.

37. Kevin Thew Forrester, interview with Sheryl Kujawa-Holbrook, January 2006.

38. A synopsis of current baptismal ministry in the Diocese of Northern Michigan can be found in the document, "Discerning Our Leadership: Bishop/Ministry Developer and the Episcopal Ministry Support Team" (n.d.)

39. Thomas Clark Ely, "Ministry Is the Life Work of All the People of God," *Mountain Echo*, March 2001.

40. Diocesan Ministry Support Team, "Deepening Baptismal Ministry in the Diocese of Vermont" (n.d.).

41. Linda L. Grenz, *Transforming Disciples* (New York: Church Publishing, 2008), 73.

42. Louis J. Luzbetak, *The Church and Cultures* (New York: Orbis, 1993), xvii.

43. Lon Oliver, "What Difference Does the Container Make?" (keynote address, conference on rural and small-church ministry, Lincoln, NE, August 2005).

44. Garret Keizer, *A Dresser of Sycamore Trees: The Finding of a Ministry* (Boston: David R. Godine, 2001), 209–10.

45. Ibid., 210.

46. Ibid., 211–212.

47. Ray, "The Small Church," in Barker and Martin, *Multiple Paths to Ministry*, 169–70.

48. Ibid., 182.

49. Stewart Zabriskie, *Total Ministry: Reclaiming the Ministry of All God's People* (Herndon, VA: Alban Institute, 1995), 90, quoted in Jenny Joyce letter to Kevin Thew Forrester, July 16, 2006.

50. Gary Shockley and Kim Shockley, *Imagining Church: Seeing Hope in a World of Change* (Herndon, VA: Alban Institute, 2009).

51. Grenz, *Transforming Disciples*, 52–53.

52. Thomas R. Hawkins, *The Learning Congregation: A New Vision of Leadership* (Louisville, KY: Westminster John Knox, 1997), 69.

53. Grenz, *Transforming Disciples*, 60–61.

54. Ibid., 59–60.

55. Jim Kitchens, quoted in Grenz, *Transforming Disciples*, 73.

56. Anton Houtepen, quoted in Robin Greenwood, *The Ministry Team Handbook: Local Ministry as Partnership* (London: SPCK, 2000), 66.

57. Eleazar Fernandez, quoted in Greenwood, *Ministry Team Handbook*, 26.

58. Elizabeth Behr-Sigel, quoted in Greenwood, *Ministry Team Handbook*, 50.

59. James V. Downton, *Rebel Leadership: Commitment and Charisma in the Revolutionary Process* (New York: MacMillan, 1973), 18.

60. Micks, *Deep Waters*, 65.

61. William Stringfellow, *An Ethic for Christians and Other Aliens in a Strange Land* (London: Wipf & Stock, 2004), 138.

62. See Greenwood, *Transforming Church*, 96.

CHAPTER 3

1. Wesley Frensdorff, "The Dream," in *Reshaping Ministry: Essays in Memory of Wesley Frensdorff*, ed. Josephine Borgeson and Lynne Wilson (Arvada, CO: Jethro Publications, 1990), 4.

2. Living Stones has twenty-six partners in the United States and Canada; see www. livingstonespartnership.org.

3. Lists of competencies for those who wish to be certified for this vocation are available through Ministry Development Network, http://ministrydevelopment.ning.com.

4. Kevin L. Thew Forrester, *"I Have Called You Friends..." An Invitation to Ministry* (New York: Church Publishing, 2003), 58–59.

5. Carol Bell, "Resolving Conflict When No One's in Charge," *The Witness*, May 1998.

6. See "A Plan for Mutual Ministry Development in the Diocese of Northern Michigan," Episcopal Diocese of Northern Michigan website, http://www.upepiscopal.org/frames/mutualframe.html.

7. For further information, see "Diocese of Northern Michigan Ministry Development: An Integral Approach," September 19, 2008, available from the diocese.

8. Early advocates of ministry development encouraged publication of a collection of his work. See David Paton and Charles Long, eds., *The Compulsion of the Spirit: A Roland Allen Reader* (Cincinnati: Forward Movement; Grand Rapids: Eerdmans, 1983). For a concise history of ministry development see Timothy F. Sedgwick, "Vision and Collaboration: Roland Allen, Liturgical Renewal, and Ministry Development," *Anglican Theological Review* 82, no. 1 (Winter 2000): 155–71.

9. Thomas Ray, "The Small Church: Radical Reformation and Renewal of Ministry," *Anglican Theological Review* 80, no. 4 (Fall 1998).

10. *The Book of Common Prayer* (1979), 855.

11. Originally issued by Forward Movement Publications (Cincinnati) in 1973, *The Celebration of Smallness* was republished by Episcopal Diocese of Northern Michigan in 1995 for its centennial celebration.

12. For a full outline of this process, see "A Plan for Mutual Ministry Development in the Diocese of Northern Michigan," Episcopal Diocese of Northern Michigan website, http://www.upepiscopal.org/Mutual%20Ministry/MMPlan.html.

13. See Marianne Arbogast, "Liberating the Baptized: Shared Ministry in Northern Michigan," *The Witness*, August/September 1994, 8–10; and Lance R. Barker and B. Edmon Martin, "Alternatives in Theological Education," A Report to the Lilly Endowment, Inc. (New Brighton, MN: United Theological Seminary of the Twin Cities, 1999), 62–68.

14. Quotations in this section are from personal notes taken by Fredrica Harris Thompsett during her October 2005 visit to Trinity Church, Gladstone, Michigan.

15. Updated information on mutual ministry in Northern Michigan provided by Ministry Developer Rayford Ray, correspondence with author, April 21, 2009.

16. Manuel Padilla, personal conversation, Ministry Developers' Cohort Retreat, Wheeling, WV, April 14, 2009.

17. Anne Tomlinson, "A Local Habitation? The Importance of Place with Today's Scottish Episcopal Church," LCM Task Group, Scottish Episcopal Church, 2007.

18. Martin Oxley and Anne Tomlinson, "Congregational Learning in Shetland, Scotland," in *Local Ministry: Story, Process and Meaning*, ed. Robin Greenwood and Caroline Pascoe (London: SPCK, 2006), 29.

19. The Theological Institute of the Scottish Episcopal Church (TISEC) offers ministerial formation in which students train for lay and ordained ministries alongside one another. Courses are ecumenically shaped and serve a number of denominations.

20. Robin Greenwood, *Transforming Church: Liberating Structures for Ministry* (London: SPCK, 2002), 86–87.

21. Elaine Cameron and Michelle Gavine, eds., *Local Collaborative Ministry: The Story So Far* (Edinburgh: Scottish Episcopal Church, 2008), 60.

22. See Isobel MacNaughtan and Tim Edwards, "Review of *Journey of the Baptised/New Century New Directions*," April 2008.

23. Cameron and Gavine, *Local Collaborative Ministry*.

24. Anne Tomlinson, "LCM Visitors Weekend: Learning from Each Other" (unpublished report of a conference at Inverurie, Scotland, September 5–7, 2008).

25. Sedgwick, "Vision and Collaboration," 155.

26. Oxley and Tomlinson, "Congregational Learning in Shetland, Scotland," in *Local Ministry*, 42.

27. Unless otherwise noted, this and other quotations from Bruce Caldwell are drawn from a video interview by Christina Carr, September 3, 2008, in Cody, WY, produced by EDS Connect for the Episcopal Divinity School and funded by a grant from the Lilly Endowment, Inc.

28. Ibid.

29. Margaret Babcock (lectures, Episcopal Divinity School, Cambridge, MA, January 7, 2009).

30. The term *environmentalist* is also used by Tim Keel, *Intuitive Leadership: Embracing a Paradigm of Narrative, Metaphor and Chaos* (Grand Rapids: Baker Books, 2008), 240–43.

31. Bruce Caldwell, interview by Fredrica Harris Thompsett, February 12, 2009.

32. "God in Rural America," video, YouTube: http://youtube.com/watch?v=8xSkoCw6jqQ. Features the story of All Saints, Wheatland, Wyoming.

33. Bruce Caldwell, interview by Christina Carr, September 3, 2008.

34. See "Area Ministry," Diocese of California, diocal.org/areaministry (accessed March 22, 2009).

35. Roland Allen, *Missionary Methods: St.Paul's or Ours?* 6th ed. (Grand Rapids: Eerdmans, 1962), 145.

36. Margaret Babcock, *Rooted in God: Moving from Maintenance to Mission*, LeaderResources, n.d.; http://leaderresources.org/rootedingod/?return=ministry.

37. *LifeCycles: Christian Transformation of Community*, LeaderResources: http://leaderresources.org/lifecycles. For information on training local mentors for *LifeCycles* groups,

see "LifeCycles," Mutual Ministry, the Episcopal Diocese of Northern Michigan, http://www.upepiscopal.org/LifeCycles.html.

38. Quoted from information on *Waterwings* at New Song Episcopal Church, Coralville, IA, http://www.newsongepiscopal.org/.

39. Cooperation with denominational seminaries in the United States and Canada is increasing. At least three Episcopal seminaries and a seminary in Canada offer short courses (a week or two) as well as online courses designed for those who are locally trained. Several of these courses were collaboratively designed with one judicatory or region in mind. They cover such subjects as baptismal ministry, preaching, pastoral care, spirituality and worship, and skills in teaching and leading groups.

40. Northern Michigan, Wyoming, and other judicatories have descriptions of various local ministries.

41. An online course led by experienced ministry developers that provides on-the-job networking is offered by EDS Connect for the Episcopal Divinity School and funded by a grant from the Lilly Endowment. The Church Divinity School of the Pacific in Berkeley, CA, and St. John's College in Winnipeg, Manitoba, Canada, also provide resources for educating ministry developers.

42. To view this effort visit Ministry Development Network, http://ministrydevelopment.ning.com/group/mdcertificateinministry development.

43. Katharine Jefferts Schori, *A Wing and a Prayer: A Message of Faith and Hope* (New York: Church Publishing, 2007), 22–23. Bishop Jefferts Schori was once Bishop of Nevada, the same judicatory where Wesley Frensdorff advocated total ministry for all the baptized.

44. Kevin Thew Forrester (oral presentation, *LifeCycles* mentor training, Berkeley, CA, January 31, 2009).

CHAPTER 4

1. Richard Gaillardetz, "Mission and Ministry," in Miller, *Lay Ministry in the Catholic Church*, 61.

2. John Smith, "The Ecclesiology of the TEAM Training Programme and Its Role in the Mission of the Anglican Church of Australia" (master's thesis, University of Notre Dame, Fremantle, Western Australia), 10–20.

3. Roland Allen, *The Spontaneous Expansion of the Church and the Causes that Hinder It.* (1912; repr. Grand Rapids: Eerdmans, 1962), 106–7.

4. Allen, *Spontaneous Expansion of the Church.* Also, David Paton and Charles H. Long, eds. *The Compulsion of the Spirit: A Roland Allen Reader* (Cincinnati: Forward Movement; Grand Rapids: Eerdmans, 1983).

5. Wes Frensdorff, interview, in Smith, "The Ecclesiology of the TEAM Training Programme," 12–13.

6. Stewart C. Zabriskie, *Total Ministry: Reclaiming the Ministry of All God's People* (Herndon, VA: Alban Institute, 1995), 9–10.

7. Louis Weil, *A Theology of Worship* (Cambridge, MA.: Cowley, 2002), 14.

8. Ibid., 14.

9. Ibid., 17.

10. Andy Crouch, "Life After Postmodernity," in *The Church in Emerging Culture: Five Perspectives*, ed. Leonard Sweet (Grand Rapids: Zondervan, 2003), 81–82.

11. Brian Farran, quoted in Robin Greenwood, *The Ministry Team Handbook: Local Ministry as Partnership* (London: SPCK, 2000), 68.

12. Smith, "The Ecclesiology of the TEAM Training Programme," 16–18; Robin Greenwood, *Transforming Priesthood: A New Theology of Mission and Ministry* (London: SPCK, 1994).

13. Jose Marins, Carolee Chanona, Teolide Trevisan, *The Church from the Roots: Basic Ecclesial Communities* (Quezon City, Phil.: Claretian, 1997), 10, 31.

14. Ibid., 30–31.

15. Rowan Williams, *Mission-Shaped Church: Church Planting and Fresh Expressions of Church in a Changing Context* (London: Church House, 2004), 48.

16. Verna J. Dozier, *The Calling of the Laity: Verna Dozier's Anthology* (Herndon, VA: Alban Institute, 1988), 114.

17. Ibid., 115.

18. Ibid., 115–16.

19. Kevin L. Thew Forrester, *"I Have Called You Friends": An Invitation to Ministry* (New York: Church Publishing, 2003), 90.

20. Kevin Thew Forrester, ed., "A Theological Framework for the Mission Strategy of the Diocese of Northern Michigan," January 29, 2009, 2.

21. Ibid., 3.

22. Ibid., 4.

23. Ibid., 4–5.

24. Ibid., 5–6.

25. Greenwood, *Ministry Team Handbook*, 11–22; Clark quote, 23.

26. Thomas C. Ely (convention address, Diocese of Vermont, Burlington, VT, November 7–8, 2008).

27. Ibid.

28. Susan Ohlidal, interview with Sheryl Kujawa-Holbrook, January 2006.

29. Ely, convention address.

30. Ibid.

31. Linda L. Grenz, e-mail to Sheryl Kujawa-Holbrook, 2005.

32. Ibid.

33. Crouch, "Life After Postmodernity," in Sweet, *Church in Emerging Culture*, 79.

34. Robin Greenwood and Hugh Burgess, *Power: Changing Society and the Churches* (London: SPCK, 2005), 104. Used with permission.

35. From *Heart in the Right Place*, 270–71, by Carolyn Jourdan. Copyright 2007 by Carolyn Jourdan. Reprinted by permission of Algonquin Books of Chapel Hill. All rights reserved.

36. Robert E. Quinn, *Deep Change: Discovering the Leader Within* (San Francisco: Jossey-Bass, 1996), xiii.

37. Greenwood and Burgess, *Power*, 161.

38. Ibid., 160–61.

39. Quinn, *Deep Change*, 166–167.

40. Ibid., 168.

41. Ibid., 168–169.

42. Peyton G. Craighill, "Seminary Education for the Ministry of All the Baptized in All Aspects of Daily Lives" (unpublished paper, July 16, 2007).

43. Weil, *Theology of Worship*, 20–21.

44. Katharine Jefferts Schori, *A Wing and A Prayer: A Message of Faith and Hope* (Harrisburg: Church Publishing, 2007), 23.

45. Steven Charleston, interview with Sheryl Kujawa-Holbrook, January 2006.

CONCLUSION

1. James Kelsey (convention address, Diocese of Northern Michigan, 2007).

2. Ibid.

3. Manuel Padilla, "Cohort Experience," April 19–23, 2009, Wheeling, WV.

4. The list of best practices was developed by the authors in consultation with ministry developers at the Cohort Experience.

5. Wesley Frensdorff, "Authority and the Theological Enterprise: An Invitation to Dialogue," in *Reshaping Ministry: Essays in Memory of Wes Frensdorff*, ed. Josephine Borgeson and Lynne Wilson (Arvada, CO: Jethro Publications, 1990), 230.

RESOURCES FOR BAPTISMAL MINISTRY

BOOKS AND OTHER PRINTED RESOURCES

Ackerman, John W. *Listening to God: Spiritual Formation in Congregations.* Herndon, VA: Alban Institute, 2001. Guide for looking at the whole of congregational life through the lens of spiritual formation.

Adams, William Seth. *Moving the Furniture: Liturgical Theory, Practice and Environment.* New York: Church Publishing, 1999. A resource for congregations interested in making adaptive changes in worship space and overall environment.

Allen, Hubert J. B. *Roland Allen: Pioneer, Priest and Prophet.* Cincinnati: Forward Movement, 1995. An overview of Roland Allen's life and ministry written by a grandson. Excerpts from Roland Allen's major works are included.

Allen, Roland. *Missionary Methods: St. Paul's or Ours?* Grand Rapids: Eerdmans, 2003. Foundational biblical vision for mutual ministry. It was first printed in 1927, re-released in 1962, and reprinted in 2003.

Allen, Roland. *The Spontaneous Expansion of the Church and the Causes that Hinder It.* 1912. Reprint, Grand Rapids: Eerdmans, 1962. A companion volume to Allen's *Missionary Methods.* Speaks to the "spontaneous expansion" of the earliest Christians as an uncontrollable force that urged them to live their faith and work for the conversion of others. Allen compares this type of church organization to modern missionary strategy. Allen believed that most church missionary efforts are weighed down in structures and procedures rather than promoting the gospel.

Bailey, Marcia. *Choosing Partnership, Sharing Ministry: A Vision for New Spiritual Community*. Herndon, VA: Alban Institute, 2007. Guide for forming ministry partnerships.

Barger, Rick. *A New and Right Spirit: Creating an Authentic Church in a Consumer Culture*. Herndon, VA: Alban Institute, 2005. Focuses on shifting the church away from consumerism and toward transformation.

Barker, Lance R., and B. Edmon Martin, eds. *Multiple Paths to Ministry: New Models for Theological Education*. Cleveland: Pilgrim Press, 2004. Affirms the need for alternative models of theological education through the stories of a wide variety of contexts, and reimagines ministry preparation for the future.

Bass, Diana Butler. *The Practicing Congregation: Imagining a New Old Church*. Herndon, VA: Alban Institute, 2004. Rooted in a belief in the possibility of transformation for mainline congregations, this book offers insights on congregational vitality, adaptability, and faithfulness. This book also offers useful perspectives on congregational histories and the varieties of tradition that can help local churches reframe their identity.

Bauknight, Brian Kelley. *Body Building: Creating a Ministry Team Through Spiritual Gifts*. Nashville: Abingdon Press, 1996. Guide to identifying and matching spiritual gifts in congregations.

Bellman, Geoffrey M. *Getting Things Done When You Are Not in Charge*. 2nd ed. San Francisco: Berrett-Koehler, 2001. A consultant working primarily in business contexts, Bellman provides practical tools for initiating change, leadership expansion, and community ownership. Ministry developers will find helpful guidance for working with shared leadership models.

Borg, Marcus J. *The Heart of Christianity: Rediscovering a Life of Faith*. New York: HarperOne, 2004. Reexamines the transformational impact of Christianity throughout history and its reemergence in the present day. A study guide to this book is also available by Marcus Borg and Tim Scorer, *Living in the Heart of Christianity: A Guide to Putting Your Faith into Action*. Incline Village, NV: Copperhouse, 2007.

Borgeson, Josephine, and Lynne Wilson, eds. *Reshaping Ministry: Essays in Memory of Wesley Frensdorff.* Arvada, CO: Jethro Publications, 1990. In this classic text, Frensdorff's still formative and vibrant passion for shared ministry is documented through his written work. Includes stories of total ministry at work in diverse settings and provocative essays on authority, education, and structural change.

Brafman, Ori, and Rod A. Beckstrom. *The Starfish and the Spider: The Unstoppable Power of Leaderless Organizations.* New York: Penguin Group, 2006. A critique of top-down leadership and an affirmation of the power of peer relationship. These authors tell stories that affirm local decentralization in business organizations. Religious leaders will find new insights and ways of looking at their local church.

Branson, Mark Lau. *Memories, Hopes, and Conversations: Appreciative Inquiry and Congregational Change.* Herndon, VA: Alban Institute, 2004. An invaluable resource on the frameworks of Appreciative Inquiry and their application to congregational self-identification.

Burt, Steven E., and Hazel Ann Roper. *The Little Church that Could: Raising Small Church Esteem.* Valley Forge, PA: Judson Press, 2000. Helpful insights and concepts for understanding small churches and the difficulties they face.

Bush, Peter George. *Where 20 or 30 are Gathered: Leading Worship in the Small Church.* Herndon, VA: Alban Institute, 2006. Best practices for worship in small congregations.

Cameron, Elaine, and Michelle Gavine, eds. *Local Collaborative Ministry: The Story So Far.* Edinburgh: Scottish Episcopal Church, 2008. Locally written vignettes, full of lively stories and images of small, struggling congregations emerging anew with imagination, courage, and renewed commitment to mission.

Collison, Brooke B. *Know and Be Known: Small Groups That Nourish and Connect.* Herndon, VA: Alban Institute, 2007. Guide to utilizing small groups as an effective means of spiritual formation and community building in congregations.

Countryman, L. William. *Living on the Border of the Holy: Renewing the Priesthood of All.* Harrisburg, PA: Morehouse, 1999. Focuses on the priesthood of the whole people of God and the fundamentally priestly nature of human life.

Croft, Steven. *Transforming Communities: Re-imagining the Church for the 21st Century*. London: Darton, Longman & Todd, 2002. Reprinted 2003, 2005. Presents a new vision for the church through building small, transforming communities within congregations.

Davis, Kortright. *Serving with Power: Reviving the Spirit of Christian Community*. New York: Paulist Press, 1999. A theological resource on the need for Christians to exercise social power as an aspect of all ministry. Useful in framing the concept of radical hospitality as well as identifying the church's role in the wider community.

Day, Katie. *Difficult Conversations: Taking Risks, Acting with Integrity*. Herndon, VA: Alban Institute, 2001. Guide to utilizing conflict creatively and as a means to enhancing understanding and relationships.

DeMott, Nancy, Tim Shapiro, and Brent Bill. *Holy Places: Matching Sacred Space with Mission and Message*. Herndon, VA: Alban Institute, 2007. Focuses on the importance of utilizing material resources to support the ministry of the congregation.

Dozier, Verna J. *The Calling of the Laity: Verna Dozier's Anthology*. Herndon, VA: Alban Institute, 1988. A collection of foundational essays focused on the theology of lay ministry and its importance in the life of the church from a respected biblical teacher.

Dozier, Verna. *The Dream of God: A Call to Return*. Cambridge, MA.: Cowley Publications, 1991. This popular and prophetic biblical educator calls laity and clergy alike to move beyond maintaining institutions and return to the everyday work of bringing about God's reign on earth. One result is a vision in which each person's ministry matters.

Dudley, Carl S. *Community Ministry: New Challenges, Proven Steps to Faith-Based Initiatives*. Herndon, VA: Alban Institute, 2002. Comprehensive handbook for congregations called to social ministries. Offers many practical tools and actual models.

Dulles, Avery. *Models of the Church: A Critical Assessment of the Church in All Its Aspects*. New York: Random House, 1976, rpt. 1986, 1987, 2000, 2002. A classic and accessible work on historical development of the basic models in ecclesiology.

Edwards, Lloyd. *Discerning Your Spiritual Gifts*. Boston: Cowley Publications, 1988. Explores spiritual gifts found in the Christian tradition and offers tools for discovering them.

Farris, Lawrence W. *Dynamics of Small Town Ministry.* Herndon, VA: Alban Institute, 2000. Guide to the geography, history, culture, and values of small town ministry.

Fenhagen, James C. *Invitation to Holiness.* San Francisco: Harper & Row, 1985. Grounds the call to be a holy person in baptism and encounters with God in the whole of human experience.

Fenhagen, James C. *Mutual Ministry: New Vitality for the Local Church.* New York: Seabury Press, 1977. An invitation to examine on a deeper level the ministry and mission of the local congregation. Emphasizes ministry as the role of the entire community, not the sole responsibility of paid professionals.

Fraser, Ian M. *Living a Countersign: From Iona to Basic Christian Communities.* Glasgow: Wild Goose Publications, 1990. An overview of the historical roots, characteristics, and struggles of basic Christian communities.

Greenwood, Robin. *The Ministry Team Handbook.* London: SPCK, 2000. Greenwood provides both practical experience and useful guidelines for the advancement of shared ministries, particularly in working with laity.

Greenwood, Robin. *Transforming Church: Liberating Structures for Ministry.* London: SPCK, 2002. Greenwood is a thoughtful author and engaging leader within the local ministry movement. As a practical theologian with more than thirty years' experience in the United Kingdom, his publications provide important grounding.

Greenwood, Robin, and Hugh Burgess. *Power: Changing Society and the Churches.* London: SPCK, 2005. Through an exploration of power, the authors offer a theology and practice that challenges churches out of inherited patterns and invites a dynamic response to God's work in the world.

Greenwood, Robin, and Caroline Pascoe, eds. *Local Ministry: Story, Process and Meaning.* London: SPCK, 2006. Valuable, encouraging, and international stories of mission-shaped churches. These reflections are important for the identity of the local church.

Grenz, Linda L. *Transforming Disciples.* New York: Church Publishing, 2008. Part of the Transformations series, this book is designed for use in congregations and examines formation and discipleship from the perspective of the church as learning community. Grenz argues that if Christians are going to move away from "being consumers of religion" to "full participation in the life of faith," we need a renewed vision of what it means to be Christian today.

Keel, Tim. *Intuitive Leadership: Embracing a Paradigm of Narrative, Metaphor and Chaos*. Grand Rapids: Baker Books, 2007. Keel's deep reflections on leadership and its theological reliance on creativity, imagination, and story are as critical for the emerging church as they are for those working in shared leadership settings.

Keizer, Garret. *A Dresser of Sycamore Trees: The Finding of a Ministry*. Boston: David R. Godine, 2001. A moving memoir written by a minister in the community of Island Pond in the Northeast Kingdom of Vermont. Compassionate and humorous, the author explores ministry and vocation as well as the role of the church in his community.

Kondrath, William M. *God's Tapestry: Understanding and Celebrating Differences*. Guides congregations through transformative processes for honoring and celebrating diverse gifts. This book takes on cultural and racial-ethnic differences and offers a process for moving past conflicts toward building healthy relationships. Provides practical tools for cross-cultural communication. Offers specific guidelines and models for multiracial communities.

Kujawa-Holbrook, Sheryl A. *A House of Prayer for All Peoples: Congregations Building Multiracial Community*. Herndon, VA: Alban Institute, 2002. Guide for congregations interested in building diversity and racial justice.

Kujawa-Holbrook, Sheryl A. *Seeing God in Each Other*. New York: Church Publishing, 2006. A collection of short essays suitable for adult education on issues related to racial justice and reconciliation, including one specifically on baptism by Fredrica Harris Thompsett.

Larive, Armand. *After Sunday: A Theology of Work*. New York: Continuum, 2004. A deep discussion of Christian work from a trinitarian perspective.

Lischer, Richard. *Open Secrets: A Spiritual Journey Through A Country Church*. New York: Doubleday, 2001. A moving first-person account of a Lutheran pastor's first years in a small rural congregation. Though intent on making changes, the young minister finds himself changed irrevocably by life in community.

Maybee, Maylanne, ed. *All Who Minister: New Ways of Serving God's People.* Toronto: Anglican Book Centre, 2001. Stories of local and shared ministry are mostly drawn from Canadian experiences. Additional advantages are attention to urban and indigenous ministries as well as excellent theological essays on the various orders of ministry, including bishops.

Micks, Marianne. *Deep Waters: An Introduction to Baptism.* Cambridge, MA: Cowley Publications, 1996. With biblical and historical reflections on water, spirit, and church, the author encourages deeper understanding about the ongoing meaning of baptism.

Mission-Shaped Church: Church Planting and Fresh Expressions of Church in a Changing Context. London: Church House, 2004. A practical handbook from the Church of England that offers advice to those interested in "fresh expressions" of the church's life as well as a framework for effective church planting.

Myers, Joseph R. *Organic Community: Creating a Place Where People Naturally Connect.* Grand Rapids: Baker Books, 2007. Practical guidance for helping churches create spaces where community naturally flourishes.

Myers, Joseph R. *The Search to Belong: Rethinking Intimacy, Community and Small Groups.* Grand Rapids: Zondervan, 2003. Discusses the yearning for belonging and for authentic community in North American culture and suggests ways congregations can evaluate and cultivate healthy community.

Olsen, Charles M. *Transforming Church Boards into Communities of Spiritual Leaders.* Herndon, VA: Alban Institute, 1995. Assists leaders in naming and celebrating the importance of ministry throughout the administrative work of the church, rather than in secular connotations.

Pagitt, Doug, and the Solomon's Porch Community. *Reimagining Spiritual Formation: A Week in the Life of an Experimental Church.* Grand Rapids: Emergent YS, 2004. A creative narrative exploring ministry and formation in an emergent church.

Palmer, Parker J. *The Courage to Teach: Exploring the Inner Landscape of a Teacher's Life,* San Francisco: Jossey-Bass, 1998. Thoughtful and encouraging wisdom on vocation and education in community. Explores the role of teaching in spiritual formation.

Paton, David, and Charles Long. *The Compulsion of the Spirit: A Roland Allen Reader.* Cincinnati: Forward Movement; Grand Rapids: Eerdmans, 1983. Reprinted 1987. A selection of Allen's works.

Quinn, Robert E. *Deep Change: Discovering the Leader Within.* San Francisco: Jossey-Bass, 1996. Explores the dynamics of deep change and its key role in revitalizing organizations.

Rendle, Gilbert R. *Behavioral Covenants in Congregations: A Handbook for Honoring Differences.* Herndon, VA: Alban Institute, 1999. Offers detailed and practical resources for congregations committed to developing congregational covenants of behavior. This book is particularly useful for congregations that have a charged emotional climate or have difficulty living into change and differences.

Robinson, Anthony B. *Transforming Congregational Culture.* Grand Rapids: Eerdmans, 2003. Discusses the role of adaptive change within the church and its impact on human transformation.

Rohr, Richard. *Everything Belongs: The Gift of Contemplative Prayer.* Rev. ed. New York: Crossroad, 2003. Rohr provides guidance in spiritual grounding that is accessible and open to all who minister in the church.

Pappas, Anthony G. *Entering the World of the Small Church.* Herndon, VA: Alban Institute, 2000. A classic work focused on the unique patterns, rituals, and relationships of the small church.

Pappas, Anthony G. *Inside the Small Church.* Herndon, VA: Alban Institute, 2002. A key resource on the mission of the small church that focuses on the unique culture and challenges of this ministry context.

Savage, Sara, and Eolene Boyd-MacMillan. *The Human Face of Church.* Norwich, UK: Canterbury Press, 2007. A handbook and training manual for leaders, integrating social psychology, organizational studies, and theology.

Sellon, Mary K, Daniel P. Smith, and Gail F. Grossman. *Redeveloping the Congregation: A How-to for Lasting Change.* Herndon, VA: Alban Institute, 2002. Focuses on developing vision and empowering teams in congregations.

Shattuck, Cynthia L., and Fredrica Harris Thompsett, eds. *Confronted by God: The Essential Verna Dozier.* New York: Church Publishing, 2006.

A collection of writings around Dozier's belief that the authority for ministry comes with baptism.

Shockley, Gary, and Kim Shockley. *Imagining Church: Seeing Hope in a World of Change.* Herndon, VA: Alban Institute, 2009. Designed to help congregations unleash imagination as a tool for creative change.

Smith, Daniel P., and Mary K. Sellon, *Pathway to Renewal: Practical Steps for Congregations.* Herndon, VA: Alban Institute, 2008. Handbook on congregational renewal—what it is and what it requires.

Smith, Huston. *The Soul of Christianity: Restoring the Great Tradition.* New York: HarperOne, 2006. A spiritual account, written by a renowned religious scholar, that explores the life and significance of Jesus in the current age.

Snow, Luther K. *The Power of Asset Mapping: How Your Congregation Can Act on Its Gifts.* Herndon, VA: Alban Institute, 2004. A helpful resource for supporting wider mission by identifying the gifts present in a congregation.

Spellers, Stephanie. *Radical Welcome: Embracing God, the Other, and the Spirit of Transformation.* New York: Church Publishing, 2006. A practical guide for churches that want to move beyond inclusivity toward hospitality that truly embraces the other.

Steinke, Peter L. *Congregational Leadership in Anxious Times: Being Calm and Courageous No Matter What.* Herndon, VA: Alban Institute, 2006. A renowned thinker on leadership offers practical wisdom for leaders dealing with emotionally charged events and consequences, and ways to move through them.

Sweet, Leonard, ed. *The Church in Emerging Culture: Five Perspectives.* Grand Rapids: Zondervan, 2003. Five Christian "thinker-speaker-writers" reflect and dialogue on what the church should look like today.

Tammany, Klara. *Living Water: Baptism as a Way of Life.* New York: Church Publishing, 2002. Baptism is at the center of this well-developed program of eight sessions for adult religious education. Poetry, art, personal reflections, Scripture, and other appropriate adornments help assure the attractive and accessible formational character of this program.

Thew Forrester, Kevin L. *"I Have Called You Friends . . ."*: *An Invitation to Ministry.* New York: Church Publishing, 2003. An introduction to the spirituality and practice of mutual ministry, including chapters on ministry development in Northern Michigan, with an emphasis on baptism and gifts for ministry and a holistic vision of shared ministry.

Thompsett, Fredrica Harris. *We Are Theologians: Strengthening the People of God.* New York: Church Publishing, 2003. Chapters provide accessible introductions to Scripture, history, theology, and ethics, each intended to encourage ongoing adult theological formation.

Tickle, Phyllis. *The Great Emergence: How Christianity Is Changing and Why.* Grand Rapids: Baker Books, 2008. Traces the major paradigm shifts in Christian history, their impact, and the hopeful possibilities for the future.

Torry, Malcolm. ed. *Diverse Gifts: Varieties of Lay and Ordained Ministries in the Church and Community.* Norwich, UK: Canterbury Press, 2006. A practical resource for local congregations to use for discerning gifts. Presupposes that all Christians are called and have gifts for ministry.

Torry, Malcolm. *The Parish: People, Place and Ministry: A Theological and Practical Exploration.* Norwich, UK: Canterbury Press, 2004. A collection of challenging short essays about local ministry. Written by parish clergy, the book covers a variety of topics, such as liturgy, pastoral care, the workplace, youth, evangelism.

Torry, Malcolm, and Jeffrey Heskins, eds. *Ordained Local Ministry: A New Shape for Ministry in the Church of England.* Norwich, UK: Canterbury Press, 2006. Examines the history, development, and practices of local ordination.

Van de Weyer, Robert. *Celtic Gifts: Orders of Ministry in the Celtic Church.* Norwich, UK: Canterbury Press, 1997. An engaging fictional version of a contemporary English diocese transformed by models of ministry with Celtic foundations. It holds an imaginative promise of what might be the shape of ministry, if everyone pursued their true calling.

Ware, Corinne. *Connecting to God: Nurturing Spirituality through Small Groups.* Herndon, VA: Alban Institute, 1997. A classic resource on spiritual formation through small groups. This book offers basic tools and advice on models of small group-based spiritual formation.

Wendland, Barbara, and Larry W. Easterling. *Spiritual Family Trees: Finding Your Faith Community's Roots.* Herndon, VA: Alban Institute, 2001. A look at the relationship between faith development and a congregation's history. This book helps congregations mine their history for insights and challenges in their present ministry.

Westerhoff, Caroline A. *Calling: A Song for the Baptized.* Boston: Cowley, 1994. An imaginative and personal collection of stories and reflections on baptism and baptismal living. Includes a study guide by John Westerhoff. Suitable for baptismal preparation and for individuals and groups wishing to reflect seriously on the themes of baptism and ministry.

Wheatley, Margaret. *Turning to One Another: Simple Conversations to Restore Hope to the Future.* San Francisco: Berrett-Koehler, 2009. Dedicated to the belief that we can change the world if we learn to talk to one another. Explores healing through conversation on a variety of levels, from personal relationships to organizational dysfunction.

Williams, Cassandra D. Carkuff. *Learning the Way: Reclaiming Wisdom from the Earliest Christian Communities.* Herndon, VA: Alban Institute, 2009. Examines the first Christian communities and offers insights on how those models can enrich congregational life today.

Wilson-Hartgrove, Jonathan. *New Monasticism: What It Has to Say to Today's Church.* Grand Rapids: Brazos Press, 2008. Makes connections between Christian community movements and the church through Scripture, ministry to the margins, economic sharing, peacemaking, and cultivating a culture of grace and truth.

Zabriskie, Stewart C. *Total Ministry: Reclaiming the Ministry of All God's People.* Herndon, VA: Alban Institute, 1995. A classic work that shares the author's reflections on the Episcopal Church in Nevada, then immersed in a total ministry model for small congregations.

WEB-BASED AND DVD RESOURCES

Alternative Worship is a comprehensive site that provides information not only on worship but also is a point of contact for the emergent church movement: http://www.alternativeworship.org/.

Center for Theology and Land. A comprehensive center at Wartburg Theological Seminary in Dubuque, Iowa, dedicated to rural ministry that offers a certificate program, conferences, resources, and more: http://www.ruralministry.com/.

LifeCycles: Christian Transformation in Community is a library of downloadable educational materials for congregations and dioceses that are grounded in baptismal ministry. The resources are useful for ongoing adult education and for training for licensed ministries, ministerial teams, and local ordination. Information available online from www.LeaderResources.org.

Local Shared Ministry is the website for an ecumenical project involving Anglican, Baptist, Methodist, and United Reformed Churches in Milton Keynes, Buckinghamshire, in the United Kingdom. The project also involves the Anglican Diocese of Oxford and other regional bodies. Includes resources and networking information. See http://webjam.com/localsharedministry.

Ministry Developers' Collaborative has materials that can be accessed on the website of the Episcopal Diocese of Northern Michigan: www.upepiscopal.org/ministrydev/.

Ministry Development: A Brief Introduction (DVD) is a general overview of the concepts and theology at the foundation of the many different expressions and processes of ministry development across the Episcopal Church. The resource was produced by EDSConnect of the Episcopal Divinity School in 2009. For more information, contact Chris Carr at ccarr@eds.edu.

The Ministry Development Network is an interactive site and the social network of the Living Stones Partnership. Provides news about events, conferences, and other resources, including a certificate for ministry developers. Available with online registration from http://ministrydevelopment.ning.com.

Mutual Ministry resources, mission strategy, and a report on "Alternatives in Theological Education" are available on the Episcopal Diocese of Northern Michigan website, www.upepiscopal.org. Click on Ministry Development, then Mutual Ministry, then Alternatives in Theological Education.

New Directions Ministries is an organization theologically grounded in creation, Christ, community, the recognition of the ministry of all baptized people, and the belief that each faith community is responsible for its own life, ministry, and mission: http://www.episcopal-church.org/smallchurch_7283_ENG_HTM.htm.

New Way of Being Church is an organization dedicated to building king-dom-shaped communities: http://www.newway.org.uk.

Small Christian Communities is an evolving global collaborative website focused on networks and resources in North America, Latin America, Africa, Asia, Europe, and Oceania: http://www.smallchristiancom-munities.org/.

Spirit of the Heartland is a site dedicated to developing total ministry in four congregations: http://www.motherflash.com/spirit/.

Thompsett, Fredrica Harris, "Wade in the Water: An Introduction to Baptismal Ministry." Available from the Episcopal Divinity School, Cambridge, MA (2007). This educational DVD and PDF study guide for adults on the history, practice, and theology of baptism can be adapted to a variety of congregational settings and formats. Informa-tion available at http://www.eds.edu/. Enter "Wade in the Water" under Search.

Total Ministry, or "A different way of 'doing church,'" is a website that provides a variety of downloads related to the theological and scrip-tural bases and implementation of total ministry. The external links section also provides information on congregations and judicatories that utilize the model: http://totalministry.org.

Total Ministry Slide Show is a resource developed by the Episcopal Dio-cese of Oregon in 1998 that describes total ministry overall, and some barriers to ministry. The slideshow is available at http://www.efn.org/~lenh/sld001.htm.

ABOUT THE AUTHORS

Sheryl A. Kujawa-Holbrook is professor of practical theology and religious education at Claremont School of Theology and professor of Anglicanism at the Episcopal Theological School at Claremont, also known as Bloy House. With Fredrica Harris Thompsett, she was the codirector of the Pastoral Excellence Project at the Episcopal Divinity School. Kujawa-Holbrook has written for *Congregations* magazine and published *A House of Prayer for All Peoples: Congregations Building Multiracial Community* (2003) with the Alban Institute. She lives with her family in California.

For the past three decades, **Fredrica Harris Thompsett**, professor emerita of historical theology at the Episcopal Divinity School, has taught and written about the ministry of the baptized. She is a member of the Ministry Developers Collaborative, on the board of *LifeCycles*, and has participated in the *Living Stones Partnership*. With Sheryl Kujawa-Holbrook, she was codirector of the Pastoral Excellence Project at EDS. Her DVD *Wade in the Water* is a popular introductory resource to baptismal ministry. She lives on Cape Cod in Massachusetts.